US Destroyers

in action

Part 2

By Al Adcock

Color by Don Greer

Illustrated by David Gebhardt and Darren Glenn

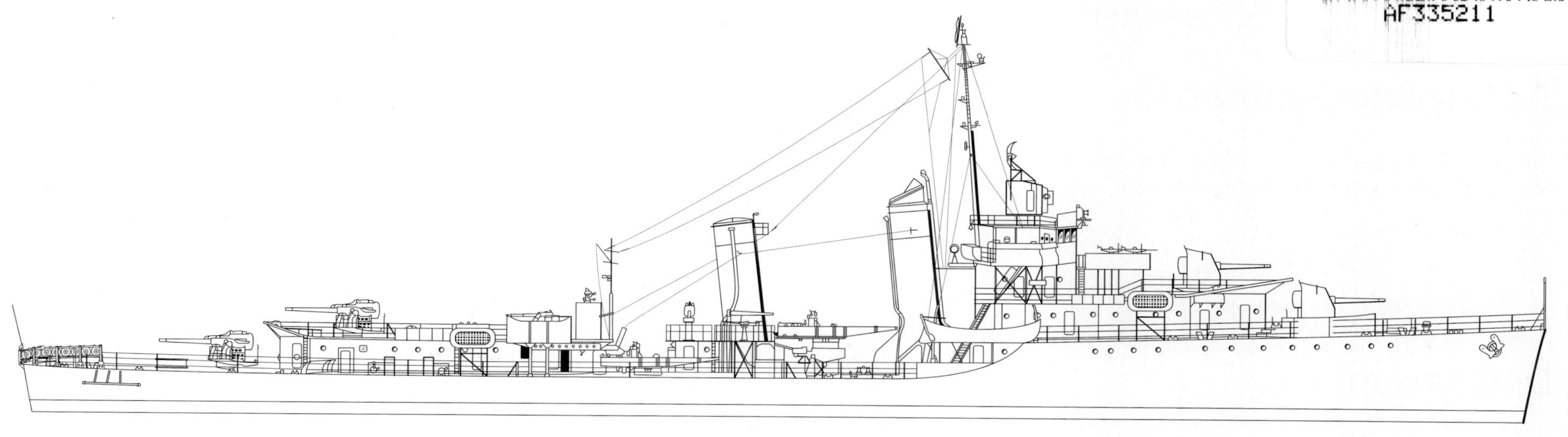

Warships Number 20

squadron/signal publications

USS MAHAN (DD-364), camouflaged in Measure 31/23D, comes under attack by Japanese *kamikaze* off the island of Leyte, the Philippines on 7 December 1944. Three of these aircraft would hit the destroyer causing fire and fatal damage to the valiant ship and crew. MAHAN became yet another casualty of the war in the Pacific.

ISBN 0-89747-467-8

If you have any photographs of aircraft, armor, soldiers or ships of any nation, particularly wartime snapshots, why not share them with us and help make Squadron/Signal's books all the more interesting and complete in the future. Any photograph sent to us will be copied and the original returned. The donor will be fully credited for any photos used. Please send them to:

Squadron/Signal Publications, Inc.
1115 Crowley Drive
Carrollton, TX 75011-5010

Если у вас есть фотографии самолётов, вооружения, солдат или кораблей любой страны, особенно, снимки времён войны, поделитесь с нами и помогите сделать новые книги издательства Эскадрон/Сигнал ещё интереснее. Мы переснимем ваши фотографии и вернём оригиналы. Имена приславших снимки будут сопровождать все опубликованные фотографии. Пожалуйста, присылайте фотографии по адресу:

Squadron/Signal Publications, Inc.
1115 Crowley Drive
Carrollton, TX 75011-5010

軍用機、装甲車両、兵士、軍艦などの写真を所持しておられる方はいらっしゃいませんか？どの国のものでも結構です。作戦中に撮影されたものが特に良いのです。Squadron/Signal社の出版する刊行物において、このような写真は内容を一層充実し、興味深くすることができます。当方にお送り頂いた写真は、複写の後お返しいたします。出版物中に写真を使用した場合は、必ず提供者のお名前を明記させて頂きます。お写真は下記にご送付ください。

Squadron/Signal Publications, Inc.
1115 Crowley Drive
Carrollton, TX 75011-5010

Acknowledgements

All of the photographs used in this publication are Official US Navy that have been declassified and provided by the following photo archivists:

Real War Photos
Floating Drydock
US Navy
United States National Archives
US Naval Historical Center

Dedication:

To all Destroyer men, you Tin Can sailors of the deep blue water; job well and truly done.

Author's Note:

The Class lineup in this book is taken from James C. Fahey's "The Ships and Aircraft of the US Fleet," 1939 Edition, the 1942 War Edition and the 1945 Victory Edition. The "little blue book" has settled many an argument concerning ships of the US Navy.

USS MAHAN (DD-364) runs at speed during a shakedown cruise in the Atlantic Ocean in 1936. Following commissioning and crew training in the Atlantic, she joined Destroyer Squadron 2 (DESRON 2), Battle Force, Destroyers at San Diego, California. MAHAN was sunk off of Leyte, the Philippines by three Japanese *kamikaze* suicide bombers on 7 December 1944. (Naval Historical Center)

364

Introduction

The Revolutionary War naval hero Captain John Paul Jones must have envisioned the destroyer when he said, *"Give me a fast ship, for I intend to go in harm's way."*

The destroyer has long been the fastest of warships, designed to protect convoys and the larger ships from harm. This vessel type was originally conceived to provide a defensive shield against surface targets; however, World War One brought new challenges in the forms of submarines and aircraft.

Following the 'war to end all wars,' the US Navy possessed the world's largest fleet of destroyers (DDs), many of which were of the 'flush deck, four pipe' type[1] constructed in great numbers during and following the 'Great War.' So many of these vessels were built that many were placed in reserve as soon as they were completed, never entering fleet service. Four of these 'flush deckers' were converted to Destroyer Mine Layers (DMs) in 1930, followed by four more in 1937, in order to utilize the hulls. Many of these destroyers were handed over to the US Coast Guard (USCG) to aid their efforts in controlling the 'rum runners' during the Prohibition era. In 1931, approximately 100 of the type were broken up to comply with the tonnage requirements enacted by the 1930 London Naval Treaty.

The 'flush deckers' were essentially obsolete by the time they were built. Their 4-inch (10.2 CM)/50 caliber[2] guns were good only for surface targets and the ships lacked sufficient anti-aircraft armament. Therefore, a new type of destroyer was required for fleet service. The need for a more modern warship resulted in the **FARRAGUT** Class of destroyers authorized in 1931-32. These vessels were designed to employ the new dual-purpose 5-inch (12.7 CM)/38 caliber gun that soon proved to be effective against either surface or aerial targets.

According to the terms of the 1930 London Naval Treaty, destroyers were limited in displacement to 1500 tons (1361 MT) and new construction of destroyers could not exceed a total of 150,000 tons. Bound by this agreement, the United States built eight FARRAGUT Class ships and they each came in at a designed 1350 tons (1225 MT) standard displacement.

The FARRAGUT Class and subsequent destroyers were armed with the quad 21-inch (53.3 CM) Mk 14 and Mk 15 torpedo tubes that carried the Mk 15 surface launched torpedo. The Mk 14 was a quad torpedo tube launcher that had an open training and firing position, while the Mk 15 launcher was fitted with a blast shield for the launching crew. The Mk 15 surface launched torpedo weighed 3850 pounds (1746 KG) and had a maximum range of 15,000 yards (13,716 M). Up to four quad launchers were fitted, depending upon the class. There were no provisions to carry reload torpedoes. When they were all launched, the destroyer had to rearm at her Destroyer Tender (AD) or at the nearest naval base. Later in the war in the Pacific, the Japanese *kamikaze* ('Divine Wind' suicide aircraft) became more prevalent while the Japanese fleet was considerably reduced in size. Anti-aircraft protection became of prime importance and many of the destroyers had some of their torpedo tubes landed in favor of 20MM Oerlikon and 40MM Bofors anti-aircraft guns.

One main advantage enjoyed by the US Navy during World War Two was radar and it began appearing on ships in the fall of 1941. The first set fitted was the SC air-search antenna, which was placed high atop the foremast and increased aerial surveillance up to 60 miles (97 KM).

[1]See US Flush Deck Destroyers in action, 4019, by squadron/signal publications.

[2]A naval gun's caliber is the barrel's length divided by the bore diameter. In this case, the 4-inch/50 caliber gun had a barrel length of 200 inches(508 CM), divided by the four-inch bore to arrive at 50 caliber.

USS ERICSSON (TB-2) cruises past either the cruiser CINCINNATI (C-7) or RALEIGH (C-8) in the late 1890s. ERICSSON was armed with a single fixed 18-inch (45.7 CM) torpedo tube in the bow and two 18-inch trainable torpedo tubes well aft, plus four 1-pounder cannon. She saw action in the 1898 Spanish-American War serving off of Cuba. (Naval Historical Center)

USS HOPKINS (DD-6) was an example of an early destroyer. Launched in 1902, she displaced 408 tons (370 MT) and was 248 feet (75.6 M) in length. Armament consisted of two 3-inch (7.6 CM)/50 caliber guns, one fore and one aft, plus four 18-inch torpedo tubes in twin mounts. The early destroyers were designed to protect the battleships from attacks from surface craft, since no submarine or aircraft threat existed. (US Navy)

The SC radar antenna was soon replaced by the improved SC-2 thru SC-5 antennas that were rectangular in shape. The SG surface-search radar soon followed and it was designed to locate targets out to 40 miles (64 KM). Identification Friend-Foe (IFF) antennas were placed on the yards to distinguish friendly from enemy aircraft as the war progressed. A few destroyers were also fitted with High Frequency-Direction Finding (HF-DF, or 'Huff-Duff') antennas to locate surfaced enemy submarines that were broadcasting with their radio.

The FARRAGUT Class was equipped with the high-pressure Yarrow boiler, which was built by Bethlehem Steel, and was among the first to introduce it to fleet service. The high-pressure boilers operated at 650° Fahrenheit (343° Celsius) and 400 pounds per square inch (PSI). This allowed for improved fuel usage and greater range. The 400 tons (363 MT) of onboard fuel oil allowed a range of 6000 miles (9656 KM). The four boilers provided steam to a pair of geared turbines generating 49,000 shaft horsepower (SHP), with each turbine turning one screw (propeller). The FARRAGUTs achieved a flank speed of 39.5 knots (45.5 MPH/73.2 KMH) on trials.

The 'between the wars' destroyers were originally armed with four 0.50-caliber (12.7 MM) water-cooled Browning M2 machine guns for anti-aircraft protection. One weapon was mounted on each bridge wing and the other two were on the aft superstructure. The 0.50 caliber gun proved ineffective and was replaced once the 20MM Oerlikon cannon became available. The later **PORTER** Class destroyers were also originally armed with the 1.1-inch (28MM) four-barrel anti-aircraft machine gun. This weapon also proved ineffective against aircraft and was replaced by the 40MM Bofors cannon in twin and quad mounts when it became available.

The camouflage paint scheme employed in the 1930s was the standard Measure 3, the Light Gray (approximately FS36320) System widely used on destroyers in both the Atlantic and Pacific Fleets. Between 1938 and 1940, various camouflage tests were undertaken out of Pearl Harbor, Hawaii. Destroyers were painted in many schemes, including Sapphire Blue (approx. FS25183), Glossy Ocean Gray (5-O, approx. FS15164), overall Black (BK, approx. FS37040), and Sea Blue (5-S, approx. FS35045). Several graded systems were also evaluated during this time. Out of these experiments came two of the major schemes used to camouflage US warships during World War Two. One was Measure 22, the Graded System of Navy Blue (5-N, approx. FS35044) and Haze Gray (5-H, approx. FS35237); the other was Measure 21, the Navy Blue System.

The 'between the wars' destroyers saw action in the Pacific from 7 December 1941 at Pearl Harbor to Japan's final capitulation in September of 1945. There were many losses among these early destroyers, including three FARRAGUT Class ships, one of the PORTER Class, six of the **MAHAN** Class, and three of the **CRAVEN** Class. Enemy action in the Pacific claimed ten of these 13 ships lost during the conflict. Following the Pacific War, the remaining destroyers of these classes were all scrapped or used as targets during atomic bomb tests. None survived to be honored as a memorial of their service to their country.

The 1060-ton (962 MT) destroyer USS WARD (DD-139) was typical of the World War One era class of ships designed as ocean escorts. WARD, camouflaged in an early 1918 camouflage style, was armed with four 4-inch (10.2 CM)/50 caliber guns, two of them in open mounts, and twelve 18-inch torpedo tubes. WARD sank a Japanese midget submarine in the early morning hours before the attack on Pearl Harbor on 7 December 1941. (US Navy)

USS DOBBIN (AD-3) was the destroyer tender for Destroyer Squadrons 1 and 3 (DESRONS ONE and THREE) with Destroyer Flotilla 1 in Battle Force, Destroyers (San Diego). Tied up along side is PHELPS (DD-360) Flagship of DESRON 1, WORDEN (DD-352), MACDONOUGH (DD-351), DEWEY (DD-349) and HULL (DD-350). Destroyer tenders provided barracks, supplies, ammunition, torpedoes, and fuel at forward bases. (Naval Historical Center)

Development

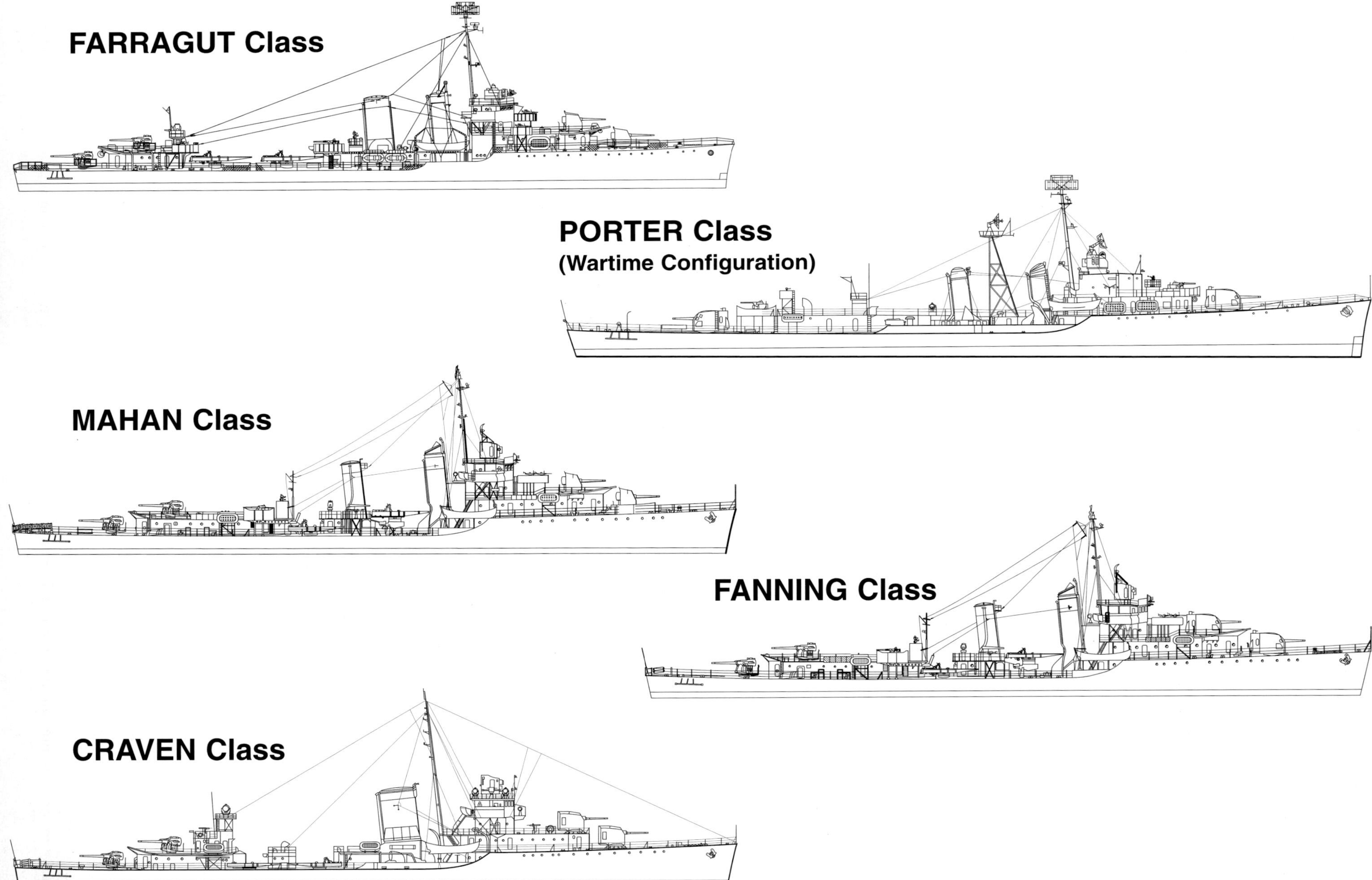

FARRAGUT Class

The eight FARRAGUT Class ships were the first modern type US destroyers constructed following World War One. These vessels were designed by Bethlehem Steel and were built by Bethlehem's Fore River yard in Quincy, Massachusetts; Bath Iron Works in Bath, Maine; and various US Navy Yards. They were built under the provisions of the 1930 London Naval Treaty, which limited newly built destroyers to a maximum standard displacement of 1500 tons (1361 MT).

Each FARRAGUT Class ship was 341 feet 3 inches (104 M) in overall length, 330 feet (100.6 M) long at the waterline, and had a beam of 34 feet 3 inches (10.4 M). Her draft was rated at 12 feet 6 inches (3.8 M) standard displacement and 15 feet 6 inches (4.7 M) maximum. Standard displacement was rated at 1358 tons (1232 MT) and the maximum war loaded displacement was rated at 2307 tons (2093 MT). With 400 tons (363 MT) of onboard fuel, her range was 6000 miles (9656 KM) at 15 knots (17.3 MPH/27.8 KMH) or 3710 miles (5971 KM) at 20 knots (23 MPH/37.1 KMH). A reported speed of 41 knots (47.2 MPH/76 KMH) was attained during trials, although this speed was probably attained in a highly lightened condition. No armor was fitted to the FARRAGUT Class, in order to keep their weight under the provisions of the London Naval Treaty.

The FARRAGUTs were originally armed with five of the 5-inch (12.7 CM)/38 caliber Mk 12 dual-purpose naval guns, with two semi-enclosed Mk 21 mounts forward and three open mounts aft. The forward gun shields were 0.125 inch (0.3 CM) thick, which was hardly considered as armor. Total weight of the assembly – including the shield and the 5-inch gun – was 15.9 tons (14.4 MT). The 5-inch Mk 12 gun had an anti-aircraft range of 37,500 feet (11,430 M) at an $85°$ elevation and a maximum surface range of 18,200 yards (16,642 M). The optically sighted Mk 33 gun director operated as the fire control system for the 5-inch weapons. For anti-aircraft protection, four water-cooled 0.50 caliber (12.7MM) Browning M2 machine guns were fitted: one each on the bridge wings and a pair on the aft superstructure. The number three 5-inch mount was replaced by either a twin or quad 40MM Bofors cannon, depending upon availability, as the war progressed. The 0.50 caliber machine guns were replaced early in the conflict by 20MM Oerlikon cannon that offered increased range and hitting power.

Other offensive armament included two quad 21-inch (53.3 CM) Mk 14 or Mk 15 quad torpedo tubes on centerline mounts between the forward and aft superstructures. There were no provisions for torpedo reloads. Two depth charge roller tracks were fitted to the fantail area with a total capacity of 14 depth charges; as with the torpedoes, no reloads were carried. Depending on the year, up to ten K-gun depth charge throwers were fitted (five per each aft deck side) to augment anti-submarine protection. Sonar (sound navigation and ranging) was fitted to aid in the underwater search for enemy submarines.

All of the FARRAGUT Class destroyers served in the Pacific and there were three losses during their four years of service during World War Two. On 1 December 1943, WORDEN (DD-352) ran aground in a storm off the Aleutian Islands and became a total loss. Both HULL (DD-350) and MONAGHAN (DD-354) were lost in the 18 December 1944 typhoon off of the Philippines.

USS FARRAGUT (DD-348) was the lead ship of the new destroyer design authorized in 1931-32. She was built by Bethlehem Steel in Quincy, Massachusetts and launched 15 March 1934. FARRAGUT was armed with five 5-inch (12.7 CM)/38 dual-purpose guns that became the standard for US destroyers through the World War Two era. She was also armed with four 0.50 caliber (12.7MM) water-cooled machine guns and eight 21-inch (53.3 CM) torpedo tubes in quad mounts, the first for a US destroyer. (Floating Drydock)

FARRAGUT is camouflaged in Measure 21, the Navy Blue System while at sea in 1943. A twin mount 40MM cannon has replaced her Number Three 5-inch mount for increased anti-aircraft protection and 20MM cannon have replaced the 0.50 caliber machine guns. An SC air search radar sits atop the foremast and an SG surface search radar is fitted just below the SC antenna. FARRAGUT earned 14 Battle Stars for her flag during the Pacific War with Japan. (National Archives)

FARRAGUT is off the Puget Sound Navy Yard, Bremerton, Washington on 29 September 1944. She is camouflaged in Measure 31/7D, a scheme that employed Ocean Gray (5-O, approx. FS35164), Haze Gray (5-H, approx. FS35237), and Dull Black (BK, approx. FS37040). The FARRAGUT Class was 341 feet 3 inches (104 M) in length and displaced 2307 tons (2093 MT) fully loaded. A fat second stack and a slimmer front stack was a recognition feature of these ships. (National Archives)

USS DEWEY (DD-349) is out on trials in the Atlantic from Bath Iron Works, Maine in 1934. She is painted in Measure 3, the light gray camouflage system that was the standard US Navy scheme for the 1930s. A crow's nest was fitted to the foremast for aerial and surface searches before the advent of radar. The two forward 5-inch mounts were semi-enclosed, while the other three mounts were of the open type. (National Archives)

FARRAGUT sits in drydock during the 1930s. This class had two screws, which was common among interwar US destroyers. The single rudder is mounted between the propeller shafts. Propeller guards mounted along the hull sides prevent wharf strikes, objects and personnel going overboard from striking the propellers. (Naval Historical Center)

(Above) DEWEY stands off of Norfolk Navy Yard, Portsmouth, Virginia on 30 March 1935. The double break to the forecastle was yet another recognition feature of the FARRAGUT Class. This class was constructed under the London Treaty of 1930, which limited destroyer tonnage to no more than 1500 tons (1361 MT). The forward stack was raised to change DEWEY's silhouette. (National Archives)

(Right) DEWEY is in the harbor in 1944, camouflaged in Measure 32/6D. This was the Medium color scheme of Light Gray (5-L, approx. FS36320), Ocean Gray (5-O) and Dull Black (BK). DEWEY was the Flagship of Destroyer Division 1, Destroyer Squadron 1. The starboard sea anchor was removed to help reduce top heaviness. (Naval Historical Center)

USS HULL (DD-350) is camouflaged in Measure 31/6D while sailing in the Pacific Ocean in 1944. She sank during a typhoon in the Philippine Sea on 18 December 1944, with the loss of over 100 officers and sailors. HULL was awarded ten Battle Stars for her service during World War Two in the Pacific Theater. (National Archives)

USS MacDONOUGH (DD-351) operates in the Aleutians during a Fleet Problem (exercise) in April of 1937. The bridge area has a vertical stripe painted on it and the Number Two stack has the upper third painted in what is believed to be red or blue to denote her assigned 'Force.' The ship is riding high in the water with a major portion of the black boot topping showing, which indicated a low fuel condition. (National Archives)

MacDONOUGH sails in calm Pacific seas in the late 1930s. The mid-deck mounted twin quad 21-inch torpedo tubes are located between the Number Three and Four open mount 5-inch/38 dual-purpose guns. No depth charge throwers (K-Guns) or roller tracks have been fitted to the stern and fantail area at this time. (National Archives)

In December of 1943, MacDONOUGH was camouflaged in Measure 21, the Navy Blue System that provided the lowest visibility to aerial and surface observers in most light conditions. Depth charge roller tracks, roller racks, and K-Guns are fitted to the fantail area. A quad 40MM cannon has replaced the Number Three open mount 5-inch gun. A bandstand containing a 20MM cannon has been erected forward of the bridge. (National Archives)

USS WORDEN (DD-352) sails out of Puget Sound Navy Yard in September of 1935. She became part of Destroyer Division 1, Destroyer Squadron 1 at Pearl Harbor. WORDEN was lost when she grounded and broke up at Amchitka Island, Alaska on 1 December 1943. She was awarded four Battle Stars for her flag for service in the Pacific. (National Archives)

MacDONOUGH comes up alongside another ship in the Pacific to exchange movies and receive mail in 1943. She is camouflaged in Measure 21, the Navy Blue System adopted for the Pacific area during 1943. The anti-aircraft defenses were improved with the addition of 20MM mounts around the bridge area and the FD radar for the 5-inch Mk 33 gun director. (National Archives)

WORDEN sails in the Pacific during the happy times before the beginning of the Second World War. A pair of depth charge roller tracks are installed on the fantail in anticipation of participating in an anti-submarine warfare exercise. The Number Three 5-inch gun is covered in canvas to protect it from the elements. (National Archives)

(Below) WORDEN stands off of Mare Island Navy Yard, San Francisco, California, sailing under barrage balloons, following her refit and wartime modification on 21 November 1942. The modifications included the removal of the main mast, replacing the Number Three 5-inch gun with a pair of twin 40MM mounts, and removing the port anchor and the four ship's boats. The camouflage scheme of Measure 21, the Navy Blue System, has been applied over the previous Measure 3, the Light Gray System. (National Archives)

5-Inch (12.7 CM)/38 Caliber Gun, Open Mount

0.50 Caliber (12.7MM) Water-Cooled Machine Gun

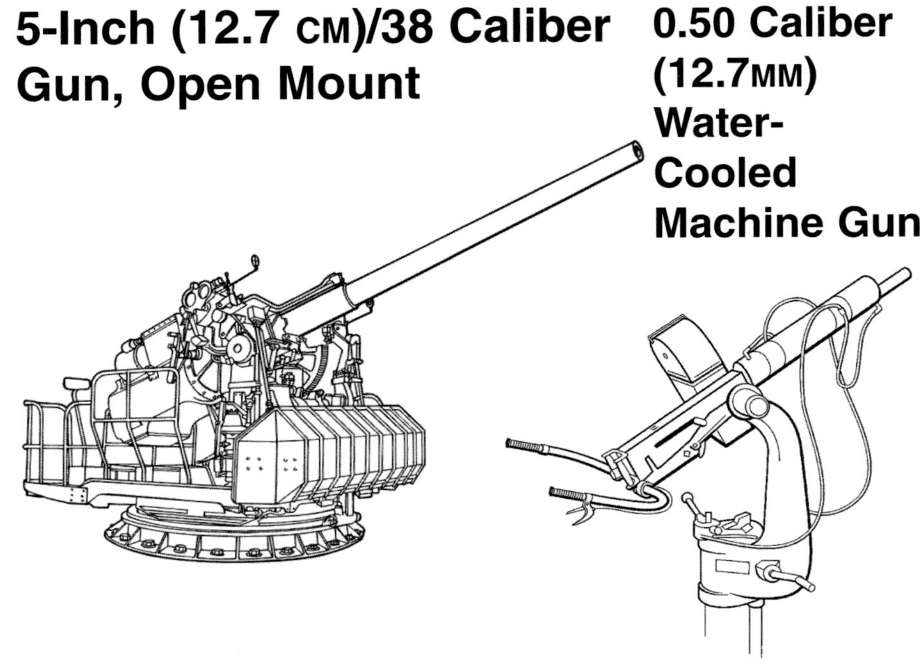

USS DALE (DD-353) was constructed by New York Navy Yard and launched on 23 January 1935. No depth charge roller tracks were installed, which indicated a time frame of 1935 to 1937. The Number One and Two gun mounts are semi-enclosed. The lighter weight open and semi-open gun mounts were a sacrifice to inherent top-heavy conditions in the class. (National Archives)

DALE is underway on 28 April 1938. She was assigned to Destroyer Division 2, Destroyer Squadron 1, Destroyer Flotilla 1, Battle Force at San Diego, California. DALE is painted in Measure 3, the standard US Navy pre-war era paint scheme. The Mk 33 gun director is fitted atop the bridge superstructure. (National Archives)

DALE is camouflaged in Measure 31/6D following a refit on 5 October 1944. The foremast contains an SC air-search radar at the top and an SG surface search radar just below it. Identification Friend-Foe (IFF) antennas are placed on either side of the halyard. The Number One and Two 5-inch gun mounts are fitted with canvas covers (bloomers) to aid in keeping out the weather. (National Archives)

With the American Flag and signal flags flying at the fore, MONAGHAN (DD-354), DALE (DD-353), and FARRAGUT (DD-348) emerge from a smoke screen during a fleet exercise in the Pacific in the late 1930s. USS MONAGHAN, like her sister ship HULL (DD-350), was lost during a typhoon in the Philippine Sea on 17 December 1944, with the loss of all but six of her crew. MONAGHAN earned 12 Battle Stars for her service in the Pacific. (Naval Historical Center)

USS ALYWIN (DD-355), in rough seas and rainy weather in the Pacific, closes up on another ship to receive mail and perhaps swap some Betty Grable movies. She is camouflaged in Measure 31/6D, the Dark Pattern System. ALYWIN is armed with four 5-inch/50 naval guns, a pair of twin 40MM cannon, and five 20MM cannon. She also has a pair of quad 21-inch torpedo tubes, depth charge roller racks, roller tracks, and four K-Guns. (Naval Historical Center)

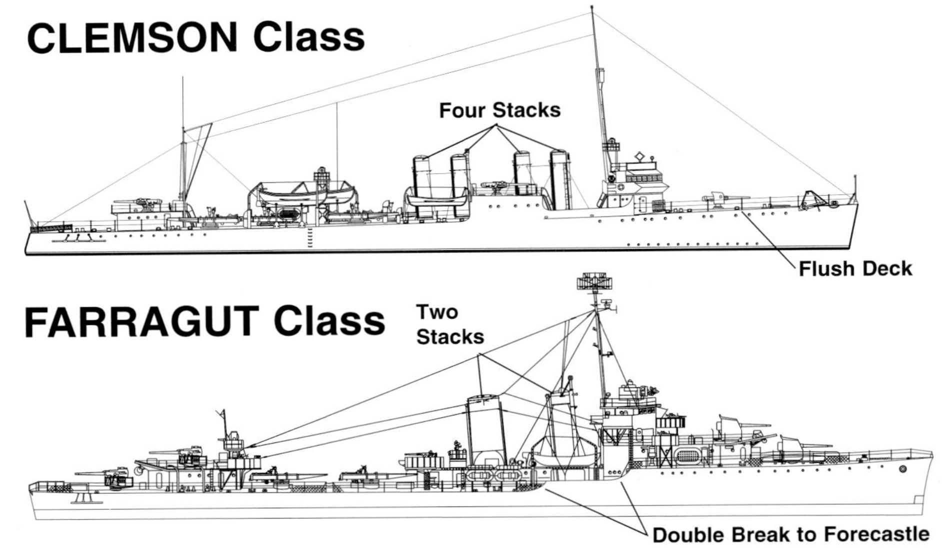

PORTER Class

The PORTER Class was conceived, constructed, and commissioned as Heavy Destroyers and Squadron Leaders. All eight ships served with the Battle Force, Destroyers originally stationed at San Diego, California. This force moved to Pearl Harbor, Hawaii in 1940, when the Japanese threat became evident.

The PORTER Class was 381 feet (116.1 M) in length and 36 feet 2 inches (11 M) in beam. Her draft was rated at 10 feet 6 inches (3.2 M) standard and 13 feet 9 inches (4.2 M) maximum war load. Standard displacement as originally stated in 1936 was 1850 tons (1678 MT), but this rose to 2154 tons (1954 MT) by the time World War Two began. The maximum war load displacement was rated at 2857 tons (2592 MT). The PORTERs rated speed of 37 knots (42.6 MPH/68.6 KMH) was achieved with four Babcock & Wilcox boilers providing steam to two geared turbines driving twin screws. Range with 635 tons (576 MT) of onboard fuel was rated at 6500 nautical miles (7485 miles/12,045 KM) at 12 knots (13.8 MPH/22.2 KMH).

The PORTERs were heavily armed for destroyers, with eight dual-purpose 5-inch (12.7 CM)/38 guns in four twin mounts: two forward and two aft. The Mk 33 optical director originally controlled these weapons until it was replaced by the radar controlled Mk 37 director. Two water-cooled 0.50 caliber (12.7MM) Browning M2 machine guns were fitted fore and aft for anti-aircraft protection. The PORTER Class was designed – and bases installed – for the 1.1-inch (28MM) quad machine guns that would be fitted as soon as they became available. When they were finally available and in service, the 1.1-inch gun was found to have inadequate firepower and proved to be unreliable. The 40MM Bofors cannon – first in twin mounts and finally in quad mounts – soon replaced the 1.1-inch machine guns. Single mounted 20MM Oerlikon cannon replaced the 0.50 caliber machine guns. A pair of quad 21-inch (53.3 CM) torpedo tubes on the ship's centerline and two depth charge roller tracks on the fantail rounded out the PORTER Class' armament. In a further attempt to reduce top weight as additional armament was added, the stacks were cut down and single pole fore and main masts replaced the tripod masts in 1941.

Japanese employment of the *kamikaze* later in the war made increased anti-aircraft protection of prime importance to the five PORTERs serving in the Pacific. The number three twin 5-inch mount was landed and replaced by a single enclosed 5-inch mount. There were now ten 40MM Bofors cannon, with a quad 40MM replacing the number two 5-inch guns. The number two quad torpedo tubes were also landed and 40MM cannon were placed in their stead. One of the depth charge roller tracks was removed to reduce top weight. SELFRIDGE (DD-357), WINSLOW (DD-359), and PHELPS (DD-360) had all torpedo tubes landed and 40MM cannon installed in their place.

McDOUGAL (DD-358), WINSLOW, and MOFFETT (DD-362) served in the Atlantic until the war in Europe ended in May of 1945. McDOUGAL and WINSLOW were then modified as radar picket ships and redesignated as AG-126 and AG-127, respectively, and sent to the Pacific war zone. Class leader PORTER (DD-356) was lost when she was torpedoed by a Japanese submarine on 26 October 1942. The destroyer was escorting the aircraft carrier HORNET (CV-8) off the Santa Cruz Islands, southeast of the Solomons.

USS PORTER (DD-356) was the lead ship in the 1933 class of eight ships. They were classified as Heavy Destroyers and assigned as Destroyer Leaders of the Battle Force, Destroyers, based at San Diego, California. The PORTER Class was armed with eight 5-inch (12.7 CM)/38 dual-purpose naval guns in four twin mounts: two forward and two aft. PORTER served as Flagship of Destroyer Squadron 2. (National Archives)

PORTER off of Mare Island Navy Yard, California on 4 November 1941, a month before the war in the Pacific began. She is camouflaged in Measure 11, the Sea Blue System. Her armament has been increased with the addition of a quad 1.1-inch (28MM) machine gun mount in the bandstand directly in front of the bridge. Her aft tripod main mast has been removed and replaced with a short gaff for the National Ensign. (Naval Historical Center)

USS SELFRIDGE (DD-357) displays her ultimate wartime armament of two twin mount 5-inch/38 guns, one fore and one aft. A single 5-inch/38 mount replaced her Number Three twin 5-inch mount. Twin 40MM mounts replaced her Number Two twin 5-inch gun forward of the superstructure and another twin 40MM was fitted on the after superstructure. SELFRIDGE is painted in Measure 32/22D, the Medium Pattern System. (National Archives)

In this restricted wartime photo, PORTER is again off Mare Island Navy Yard following a refit that included a camouflage paint scheme of Measure 21, the Navy Blue System. She was fitted with a twin 40MM mount to replace the ineffective quad 1.1-inch machine gun and a Mk 37 Fire Control with FD radar. A Japanese submarine sank PORTER during the Battle of Santa Cruz, off Guadalcanal, on 26 October 1942. (National Archives)

Mk 32 5-Inch (12.7 CM)/38 Caliber Dual Mount

(PHELPS and SELFRIDGE only, after modernization)

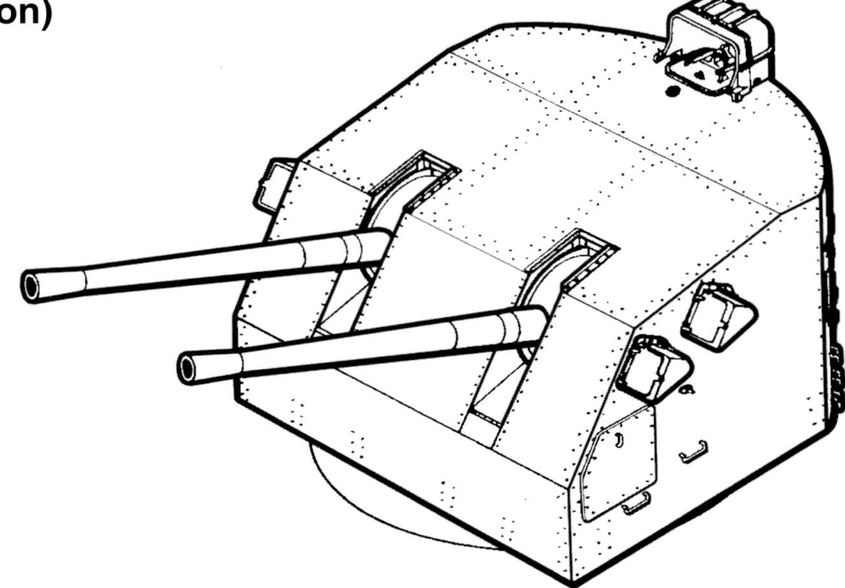

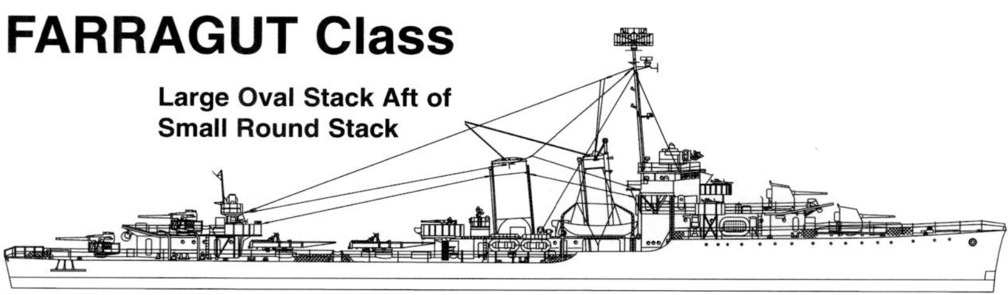

USS McDOUGAL (DD-358) lies off of Staten Island, New York just before her commissioning in 1936. Her gun directors and rangefinders have yet to be installed atop the bridge. The main tripod mast contains a pair of searchlights and a lookout position.

McDOUGAL eventually became the Flagship of Destroyer Division 17, Battle Force, Destroyers at San Diego. (National Archives)

FARRAGUT Class

Large Oval Stack Aft of
Small Round Stack

PORTER Class
(Wartime Configuration as Radar Picket)

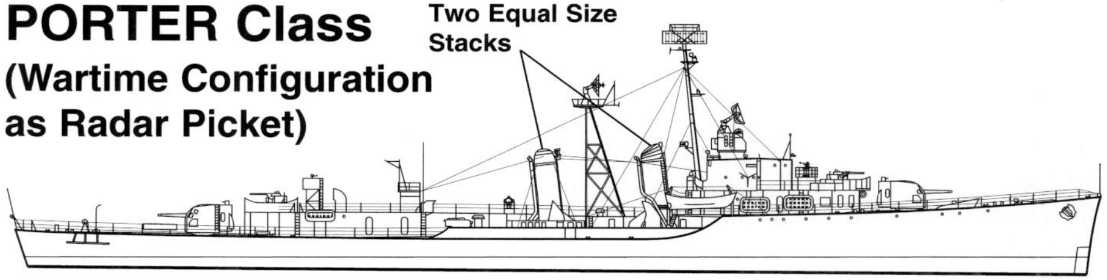

Two Equal Size Stacks

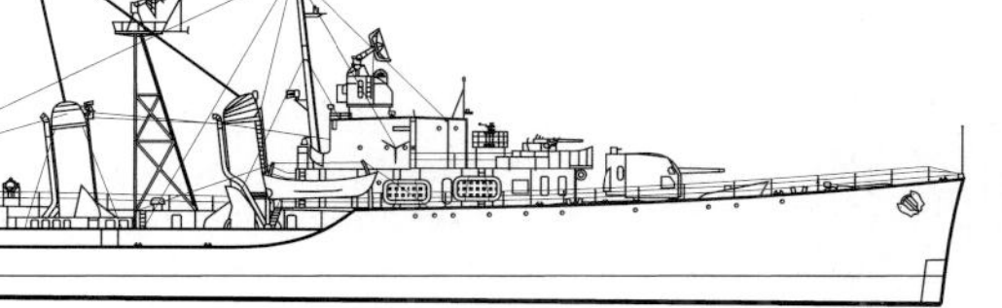

Two quad 21-inch torpedo tubes and torpedo directors are situated on SELFRIDGE's mid-deck area in the late 1930s. Ready rounds of torpedoes were housed in the containers on the main deck below the torpedo directors. Her Number One stack has been fitted with a cowl to direct the stack gases up and aft of the bridge superstructure. (National Archives)

McDOUGAL is moored alongside HMS PRINCE of WALES in Placentia Bay, Newfoundland, Canada in August of 1941. The destroyer transferred President Franklin D. Roosevelt to the British battleship for a meeting with Prime Minister Winston Churchill to discuss terms of the Atlantic Charter. McDOUGAL is camouflaged in Measure 12, the early Graded System that consisted of Sea Blue (5-S, approx. FS35045) and Ocean Gray (5-O). The relative size of the US destroyer and the British battleship is apparent. (Naval Historical Center)

USS PHELPS (DD-360) makes 29.56 knots (34 MPH/55 KMH) on Run Number 18 North during qualification trials off Rockland, Maine on 17 December 1935. Her 'government furnished' 5-inch gun mounts, torpedo tubes, and gun directors have not been installed. The PORTER class was credited with a maximum speed of 37 knots (42.6 MPH/68.6 KMH). PHELPS became the Flagship for Destroyer Squadron 1. (National Archives)

PHELPS sails out of Charleston Harbor, South Carolina following a refit in November of 1944. This included a modified bridge area and replacing the Number Two twin 5-inch mount with a quad mount 40MM cannon. Additionally, a pole main mast with an HF/DF antenna to detect submarine radio transmissions was installed and she was repainted in Measure 32/3D, the Medium paint scheme. The Number Three twin 5-inch mount was replaced with a single 5-inch/38 gun to bolster anti-aircraft defenses. (National Archives)

PHELPS is off of San Francisco, California on 11 December 1942. She has the mid-war armament change that consisted of a twin 40MM mount between the Number Two 5-inch twin mount and the bridge and three twin 40MM mounts, including one replacing the Number Three 5-inch twin mount. PHELPS is camouflaged in Measure 21, the Navy Blue System. (Naval Historical Center)

USS CLARK (DD-361) escorts a Pacific-bound convoy near the Panama Canal Zone on 26 May 1943. She is camouflaged in Measure 21, the Navy Blue System. Anti-aircraft armament consists of four twin 40MM mounts – one forward and three aft – and five 20MM cannon in single mounts. Mk 51 gun directors controlled the 40MM cannon. (Naval Historical Center)

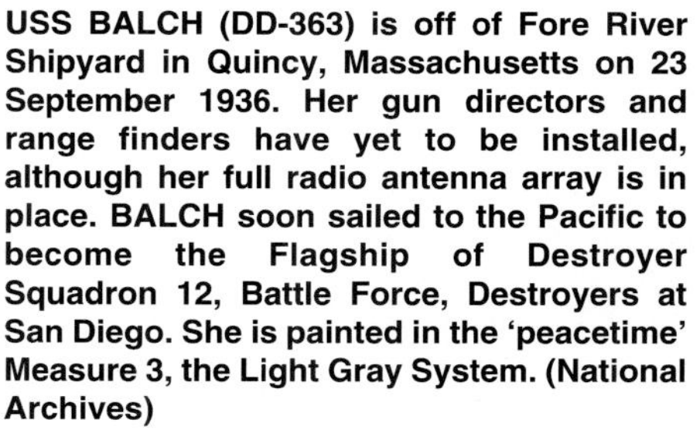

USS BALCH (DD-363) is off of Fore River Shipyard in Quincy, Massachusetts on 23 September 1936. Her gun directors and range finders have yet to be installed, although her full radio antenna array is in place. BALCH soon sailed to the Pacific to become the Flagship of Destroyer Squadron 12, Battle Force, Destroyers at San Diego. She is painted in the 'peacetime' Measure 3, the Light Gray System. (National Archives)

BALCH (DD-363) stands by as the aircraft carrier YORKTOWN (CV-5) is abandoned by her crew on 4 June 1942. Two Japanese Type 91 aerial torpedoes hit the carrier during the Battle of Midway. The US lost YORKTOWN during the battle, while the Japanese lost four of their carriers. (US Navy)

1.1-inch (28MM) Quad Mount Machine Gun

(Below) BALCH sails off of San Francisco on 30 August 1943. She carries SC air search radar atop her foremast, an SG surface search radar just below, and IFF antennas at either side of the yards. She is camouflaged in Measure 21, the Navy Blue System. BALCH was Flagship for Destroyer Squadron 12, Battle Force, Destroyers San Diego in the late 1930s. (Naval Historical Center)

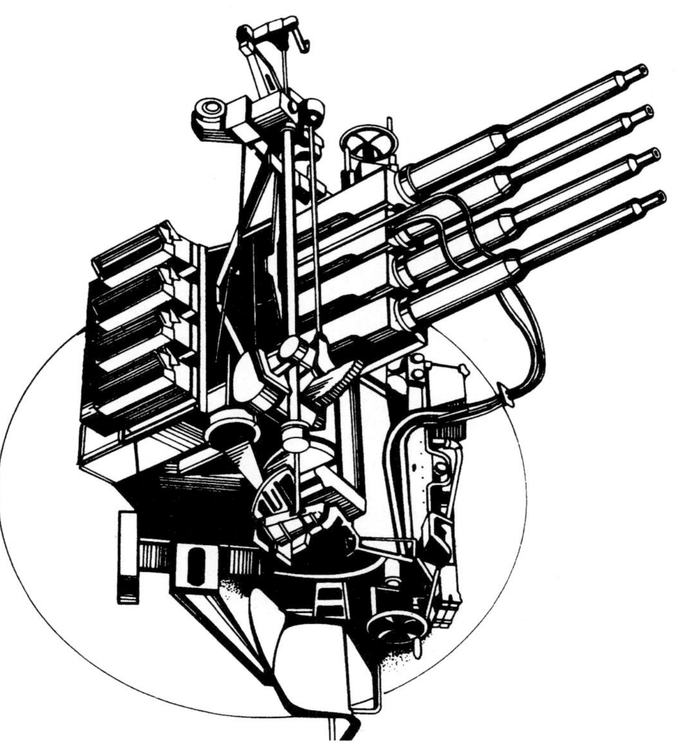

MAHAN Class

The MAHAN Class was an improved FARRAGUT Class with a slight increase in beam, a single break to the forecastle, and an increase in torpedo tubes. The most important improvements were in the boilers and engine department.

The MAHAN Class was 341 feet 8 inches (104.1 M) in length, with a beam of 35 feet 6 inches (10.8 M). This beam is 1 foot 3 inches (0.4 M) wider than the FARRAGUT's 34 foot 3 inch (10.4 M) beam. MAHAN's draft was rated at 9 feet 10 inches (3 M) standard and 13 feet 10 inches (4.2 M) full war load. Its displacement was initially 1500 tons (1361 MT) to comply with the 1930 London Naval Treaty. The standard displacement later rose to 1700 tons (1542 MT) when additional electronic and defensive weapons were added, and the full war load displacement was 2329 tons (2113 MT).

Her standard armament consisted of five 5-inch (12.7 CM)/38 dual-purpose guns, with two semi-enclosed forward mounts and three fully open aft mounts. Two of the aft mounts were placed on the aft superstructure and the number five mount was located on the fantail. The standard torpedo armament was increased from eight to 12 total tubes in three quad mounts. The forward tubes were mounted on a centerline pedestal between the stacks and the two aft quad tubes were located on the deck edge between the aft stack and the aft superstructure. Her anti-aircraft armament initially consisted of four 0.50 caliber (12.7MM) Browning M2 water-cooled machine guns. British experiences in the war in Europe from 1939 to 1941 and the US at Pearl Harbor prompted the US Navy to bolster defensive armament. Consequently, a pair of 20MM Oerlikon cannon replaced the number three 5-inch gun, with four other cannon placed around the bridge area. By 1944, the pair of 20MM guns that had replaced the number three 5-inch gun were themselves replaced by a pair of twin 40MM Bofors cannon. Bolstered defenses against *kamikaze* (suicide aircraft) attacks were ultimately employed on LAMSON (DD-367) and SHAW (DD-373) with the replacement of all torpedo tubes by 40MM cannon.

The MAHAN Class was fitted with a Mk 33 optical fire control system on the bridge roof. This device controlled the number one and two 5-inch guns. By 1942, both SC air search radar and Mk 4 gunnery radar were added, followed by the SG surface search radar in 1943. Mk 51 directors were fitted to control the added 40MM guns. The fantail was fitted with two depth charge roller tracks that would be utilized against underwater threats being tracked by the onboard sonar.

The MAHANs were fitted with advanced boilers and machinery designed by the firm of Gibbs & Cox. These ships utilized Babcock & Wilcox boilers that operated at 700° Fahrenheit (371° Celsius) and high-pressure double reduction geared General Electric turbines driving twin screws and providing 49,000 SHP. This gave the MAHANs a 36.5 knot (42 MPH/67.6 KMH) flank speed. A range of 6500 nautical miles (7485 miles/12,045 KM) was possible at 12 knots (13.8 MPH/22.2 KMH) with 522 tons (474 MT) of onboard fuel.

Eight of the 16 MAHAN Class ships built were lost to action in the Pacific. CASSIN (DD-372), DOWNES (DD-375), and SHAW (DD-373) were severely damaged when the Japanese attacked Pearl Harbor on 7 December 1941. The machinery and armament from CASSIN and DOWNES was salvaged and installed in new hulls constructed at Mare Island Navy Yard in San Francisco, California and given their old hull numbers. SHAW was also rebuilt at Mare Island and was available for service in time to see action in the Battle of Santa Cruz in October of 1942. TUCKER (DD-374) was lost off of Espiritu Santo on 4 August 1942, when she strayed into a newly seeded US minefield whose location was unknown to TUCKER's commanding officer. This mishap cost the ship and six of her crew. CUSHING (DD-376) and PRESTON (DD-379) were both lost during the First and Second Battles of Guadalcanal in

USS MAHAN (DD-364) was the lead ship of the 1933 Class of 16 destroyers. She was built by United Dry Dock Company, Bethlehem, Staten Island, New York and launched on 15 October 1935. She is camouflaged in Measure 3, the Light Gray System. The MAHAN Class was armed with five 5-inch (12.7 CM)/38 dual-purpose naval guns, two forward in semi-enclosed mounts and three aft in open mounts. (Naval Historical Center)

MAHAN and a sister maneuver during the Battle of the Santa Cruz Islands on 26 October 1942. MAHAN was sunk off of Leyte, the Philippines on 7 December 1944, when Japanese *kamikaze* aircraft attacked her. Three of them crashed into MAHAN, causing mortal damage. She was camouflaged in Measure 21 in 1942 while operating in Destroyer Division 3, out of Pearl Harbor, Hawaii. (Naval Historical Center)

DRAYTON (DD-366) takes part in a camouflage experiment at Pearl Harbor in 1941. She is painted in a Sapphire Blue (approx. FS25183) paint scheme overall, with the top of the foremast painted in Light Gray (5-L). A North American SNJ trainer assigned the duty of aerial observer and photographic aircraft photographed DRAYTON. After the application of this bright blue paint, DRAYTON was nicknamed the 'Blue Beetle.' (Naval Historical Center)

MAHAN is camouflaged in Measure 31/23D as she sails off the Mare Island Navy Yard, California on 21 June 1944. She carries four 5-inch/38 guns, six 40MM cannon, and eight 20MM cannon in single mounts. The three quad torpedo tubes were retained during her wartime service, but were never utilized. MAHAN was awarded five Battle Stars for her flag for her Pacific service during World War Two. (National Archives)

November of 1942. They were operating with Rear Admiral Willis 'Ching' Lee's and Rear Admiral Daniel Callaghan's Battleship Force during those engagements. The class leader MAHAN (DD-364) was sunk off of Leyte, the Philippines on 7 December 1944, when she was attacked by 12 *kamikaze* fighter and bomber aircraft. Her gunners were able to shoot down several attackers, but three made it through the anti-aircraft fire and in quick succession crashed into the valiant destroyer, the bombs and ensuing fire doomed MAHAN. Miraculously, only one officer and five 'bluejackets' (enlisted sailors) were killed in the attack. REID (DD-369) suffered the same fate four days later, when two *kamikazes* struck her off of Limasawa Island, the Philippines, taking over 50 of her crew with her. REID was the last loss of a MAHAN Class destroyer in the Pacific and she had earned seven Battle Stars for her flag.

The MAHAN Class served with great distinction during their operations in the Pacific escort-

Single Mount
20MM Cannon

Twin Mount
40MM Cannon

Quad Mount
40MM Cannon

USS CONYNGHAM (DD-371) at sea with REID (DD-369) in the center and CLARK (DD-361) to the far right during maneuvers from Pearl Harbor, Hawaii in the late 1930s. The destroyers were part of Destroyer Squadron 3, with CLARK as the Flagship. All of the destroyers are fitted with depth charge roller tracks and the Number Four and Five 5-inch mounts on the nearest ships are pointed skyward in anticipation of a mock air attack. (Naval Historical Center)

USS REID (DD-369) moves at speed in the Pacific during the late 1930s. She is camouflaged in Measure 3, the Light Gray System. REID was sunk while cruising off of Limasawa Island, Leyte by a pair of Japanese *kamikazes* on 11 December 1944, taking over 50 of her crew to the bottom of the Pacific. REID was awarded seven Battle Stars for her flag. (Naval Historical Center)

ing the 'big boys' – carrier Task Forces and amphibious groups – during the four years of war. Following hostilities, all remaining MAHANs were cut up between 1946 and 1948; none escaped the scrapper's torch.

Flying the Federal Shipbuilding house flag at the foremast, USS FLUSSER (DD-368) undergoes trials in the Atlantic in 1935. Following commissioning and training, she joined Destroyer Division 3 at San Diego, California. During the Japanese attack on Pearl Harbor on 7 December 1941, FLUSSER was part of the escort for the aircraft carrier LEXINGTON (CV-2), which was returning from Midway Island. They became part of the Task Force assigned to try and hunt down the attacking Imperial Japanese Fleet. FLUSSER was awarded eight Battle Stars for her flag for her service in the Pacific. (Naval Historical Center)

USS CASSIN (DD-372) stands off of the Philadelphia Navy Yard in February of 1937. She is camouflaged in Measure 3, the Light Gray System. Following commissioning and training in the Pacific, she joined Destroyer Division 5, first at San Diego, then Pearl Harbor, Hawaii. CASSIN was armed with five 5-inch/38 guns, four 0.50 caliber (12.7mm) water-cooled machine guns, and 12 torpedo tubes in three quad mounts. (National Archives)

CONYNGHAM (DD-371) closes up on another destroyer to transfer mail and the latest movies in 1941. She appears to be camouflaged in Measure 1, the Dark Gray System, with the mast from the bridge superstructure and up painted light gray (5-L). CONYNGHAM was awarded 14 Battle Stars for her Pacific service. (Naval Historical Center)

MAHAN Class, 1938

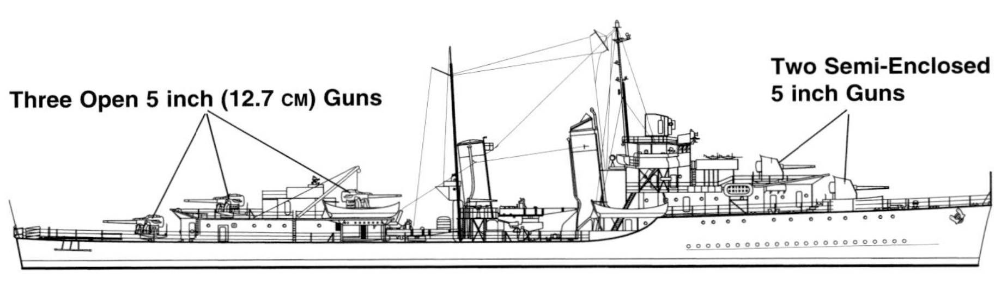

MAHAN Class, 1943

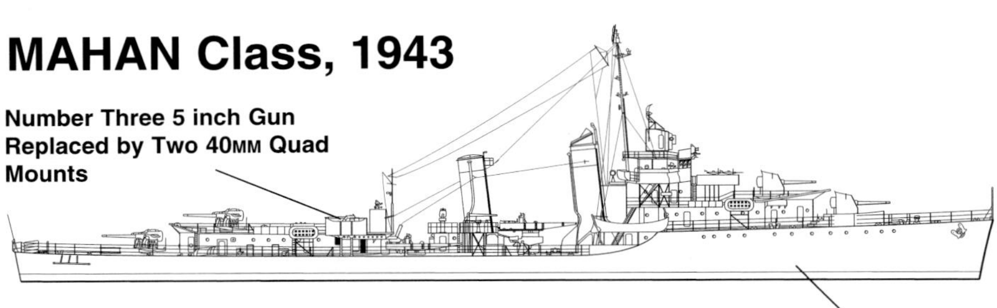

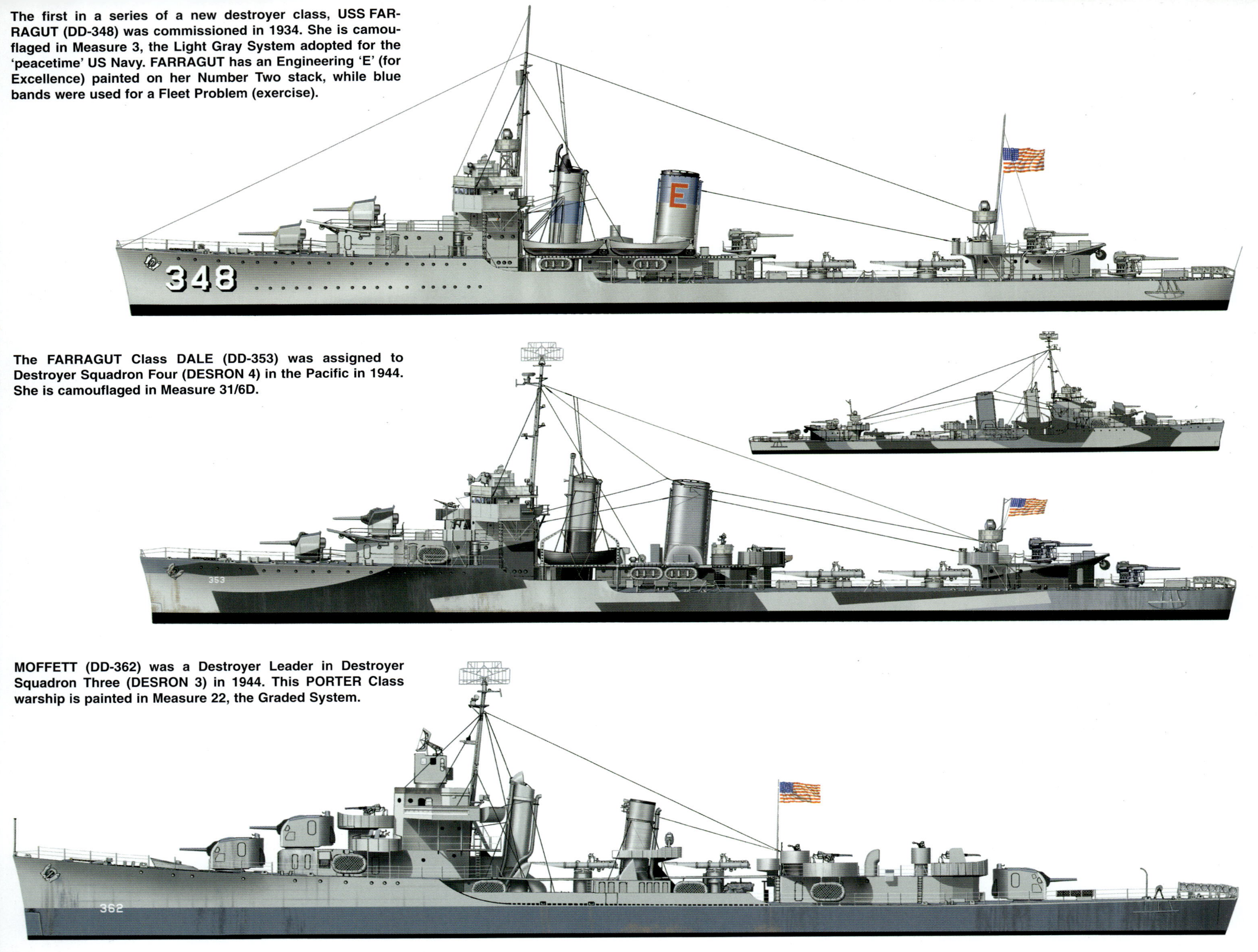

The first in a series of a new destroyer class, USS FAR-RAGUT (DD-348) was commissioned in 1934. She is camouflaged in Measure 3, the Light Gray System adopted for the 'peacetime' US Navy. FARRAGUT has an Engineering 'E' (for Excellence) painted on her Number Two stack, while blue bands were used for a Fleet Problem (exercise).

The FARRAGUT Class DALE (DD-353) was assigned to Destroyer Squadron Four (DESRON 4) in the Pacific in 1944. She is camouflaged in Measure 31/6D.

MOFFETT (DD-362) was a Destroyer Leader in Destroyer Squadron Three (DESRON 3) in 1944. This PORTER Class warship is painted in Measure 22, the Graded System.

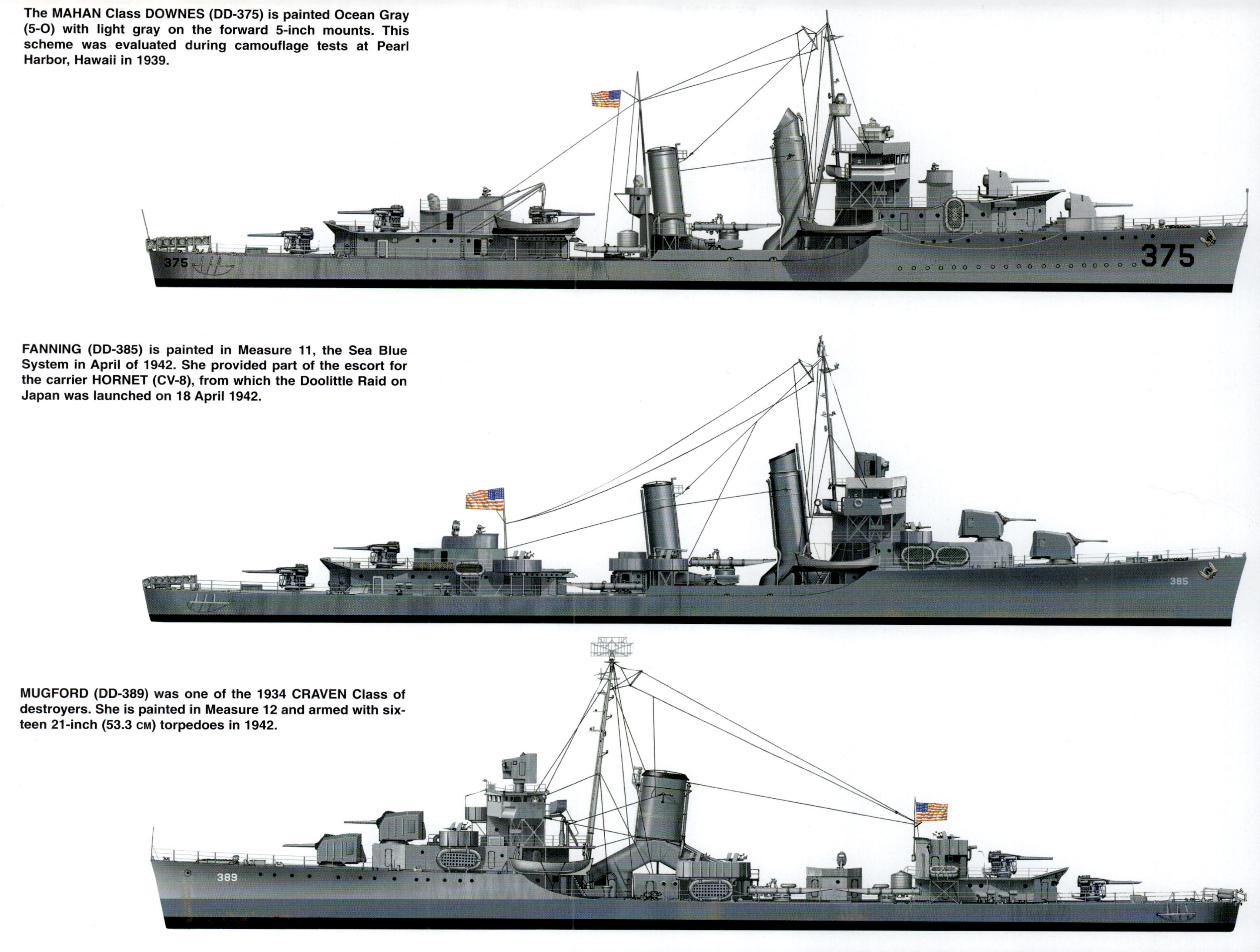

The MAHAN Class DOWNES (DD-375) is painted Ocean Gray (5-O) with light gray on the forward 5-inch mounts. This scheme was evaluated during camouflage tests at Pearl Harbor, Hawaii in 1939.

FANNING (DD-385) is painted in Measure 11, the Sea Blue System in April of 1942. She provided part of the escort for the carrier HORNET (CV-8), from which the Doolittle Raid on Japan was launched on 18 April 1942.

MUGFORD (DD-389) was one of the 1934 CRAVEN Class of destroyers. She is painted in Measure 12 and armed with sixteen 21-inch (53.3 cm) torpedoes in 1942.

CASSIN (DD-372) sails in the Pacific in December of 1939. She is painted in Measure 3, the Light Gray paint scheme. The Mk 33 optical gun director is covered with canvas to protect the sensitive optics and to cover it from prying eyes. A cowl has been added to the Number One mast to redirect stack gases. The 1.1-inch (28MM) quad machine gun has not yet been fitted in the mount in front of the bridge. (National Archives)

On 7 December 1941, CASSIN was in dry dock at Pearl Harbor when she was attacked with bombs that knocked her off of her blocks and she rolled over onto DOWNES (DD-375). CASSIN was salvaged, refloated, and towed to Mare Island Navy Yard, California, where her valuable machinery and armament were installed in a new hull. She was recommissioned in February of 1944 with the same DD-372 hull number and called the 'new' CASSIN. With new life breathed into her, she began to take the fight to the Japanese, earning herself six Battle Stars in the process. (National Archives)

Following her recomissioning ceremonies in February of 1944, CASSIN set sail for the Pacific war zone. She is camouflaged in Measure 21, the Navy Blue System that proved to provide the lowest visibility to aerial observers, such as the Japanese *kamikaze*. CASSIN is now armed with four 5-inch/38 guns, a single quad 40MM mount, and eight 20MM cannon. The port anchor was landed as a further weight reduction measure. (National Archives)

(Above) USS SHAW (DD-373) stands off of the Philadelphia Navy Yard, Pennsylvania following refitting on 26 January 1937. This ship then engaged in more training exercises in the Atlantic. She is fitted with an Mk 33 optical gun director on the roof of the bridge area. Following another refit at Mare Island Navy Yard, SHAW joined the Pacific Fleet at Pearl Harbor, Hawaii. (National Archives)

(Left) Sailors prepare to 'man the rails' as SHAW enters Rio de Janeiro harbor, Brazil during the late 1930s. She was acting as an escort on a training cruise in the Atlantic with the aircraft carrier ENTERPRISE (CV-6). SHAW has the modified cowl on the Number One stack and is equipped with the tripod mast. She is painted in Measure 3, the Light Gray peacetime scheme. (National Archives)

SHAW is docked at Mare Island Navy Yard to have her temporary bow replaced with a permanent one. She was salvaged at Pearl Harbor following the Japanese attack on 7 December 1941 and towed to Mare Island Navy Yard for reconstruction. SHAW lost her bow when her forward 5-inch magazine exploded following a bomb attack. She was fitted with a new bow, bridge, and 5-inch guns and returned to service in June of 1942. (National Archives)

SHAW transfers survivors from PORTER (DD-356) to the battleship SOUTH DAKOTA (BB-57), following the Destroyer Leader's sinking during the Battle of Santa Cruz Island on 26 October 1942. SHAW is fitted with a pair of 20MM Oerlikon cannon in the bandstand mount in front of the bridge area. She has semi-enclosed mount 5-inch/38 guns on her forward deck. (National Archives)

SHAW off of the Mare Island Navy Yard on her way to the Pacific War Zone on 5 August 1945. All of her torpedo tubes have been landed and replaced with side-by-side quad 40MM Bofors anti-aircraft cannon. SHAW is camouflaged in Measure 21, the Navy Blue system and the American ensign is flying at a gaff on the number two stack. Her radar suite consists of SC air-search and SG surface-search antennas. (National Archives)

(Above) USS DOWNES (DD-375) moves in a rough cross-sea in 1938. Her Mk 33 optical gun director is covered with canvas to protect it from the salt water. The Philadelphia Navy Yard built DOWNES, which was then commissioned and trained in the Atlantic. She was then posted with Destroyer Division 5, now home ported at Pearl Harbor. (National Archives)

(Left) DOWNES at sea in 1939 with an experimental camouflage scheme of a glossy Ocean Gray (5-0) hull. Her forward 5-inch mounts and aft open mount canvas covers are a light gray. The hull number is in a non-standard black. DOWNES was painted glossy black and in a multi-color gray scheme during the 1938-1940 camouflage experiments at Pearl Harbor. (National Archives)

DOWNES departs Mare Island Navy Yard on 8 December 1943, following the refitting of her salvaged machinery and weaponry in an entirely new hull. DOWNES and CASSIN (DD-372) were both in a floating dry dock at Pearl Harbor when Japanese bombs hit them.

DOWNES' forward 5-inch/38 guns bombard Marcus Island on 9 October 1944. The loader and gun captain are fitted with protective clothing and gear and all personnel are wearing steel helmets. The 5-inch guns are elevated at approximately a 30° angle for medium range fire. DOWNES earned four Battle Stars for her service in the Pacific. (National Archives)

DOWNES is painted in Measure 21, the Navy Blue System. A pair of quad 40MM cannon has replaced her Number Three 5-inch mount. (National Archives)

USS CUSHING (DD-376) is in San Diego harbor, California in 1938. She is painted in Measure 3, the Light Gray System. Both the vertical stripe on the bridge face and the band around her number Two stack are believed to be either blue or red. CUSHING was the flagship of Destroyer Division 4 that was home ported at San Diego as part of Destroyers, Battle Force. (National Archives)

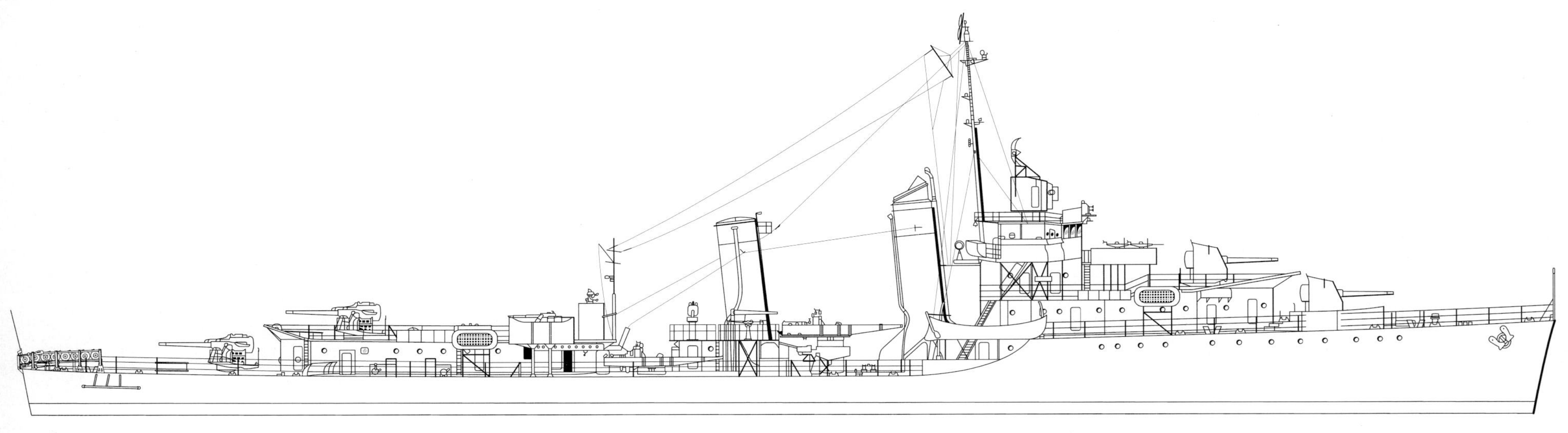

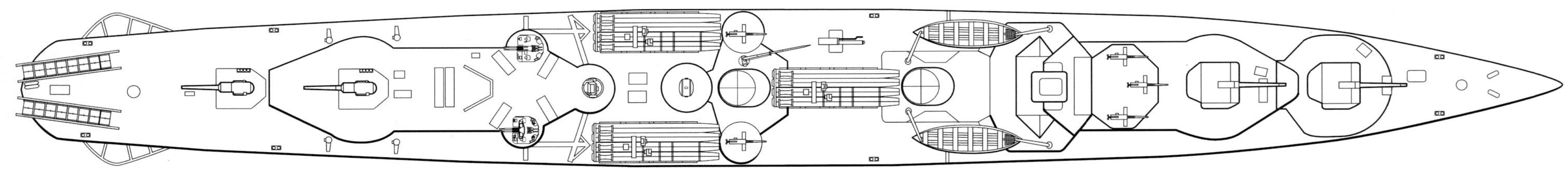

USS CUSHING (DD-376) Specifications

Overall Length:................341 feet 8 inches (104.1 м)
Beam:..............................35 feet 6 inches (10.8 м)
Draft:...............................13 feet 10 inches (4.2 м) at full load
Standard Displacement:.1700 tons (1542 мт)
Full Load Displacement:.2329 tons (2113 мт)
Machinery:.......................General Electric geared turbines, 49,000 SHP, twin screws
Speed:.............................36.5 knots (42 MPH/67.6 KMH)

Range:.............................6500 nautical miles (7485 miles/12,045 KM) at 12 knots (13.8 MPH/22.2 KMH)
Compliment:....................158
Armament:.......................Five 5-inch (12.7 CM)/38 caliber dual purpose guns in single mounts, four 20MM Oerlikon cannon in single mounts, 12 21-inch (53.3 CM) torpedo tubes in three quad mounts, two depth charge roller tracks on the fantail

USS SMITH (DD-378) is off the Mare Island Navy Yard following a refit and application of camouflage Measure 31/23D on 12 June 1944. She has the SC air-search and SG surface-search radar antennas at her foremast. A pair of quad 40MM Bofors mounts has replaced the Number Three 5-inch open gun mount. SMITH is fitted with two depth charge roller tracks on the fantail and roller racks on the deck just below the Number Four 5-inch gun. (National Archives)

SMITH takes on fuel from the battleship SOUTH DAKOTA (BB-57) on 28 October 1942, following the Battle of Santa Cruz. Two days before, a Japanese Nakajima B5N 'Kate' torpedo-bomber attacked SMITH and severely damaged the destroyer from the bridge area forward. Although burning and wounded, SMITH fought off other attacking Japanese aircraft, earning herself and her crew a Presidential Unit Citation for their actions. (National Archives)

USS PRESTON (DD-379) was the last of the MAHAN Class of 1500-ton (1361 MT) destroyers. PRESTON was the second destroyer built at the new Mare Island Navy Yard, with SMITH (DD-378) being the first. Upon completion, training, and work-up, PRESTON joined Destroyer Division 4 at Pearl Harbor, Hawaii. Like the other destroyers of Division 4, she has a vertical stripe on the face of the bridge and a painted band on the Number Two stack, both believed to be either red or blue. (National Archives)

FANNING Class

The two FANNING Class ships of 1934 were called the 'odd sisters' since they retained the 12 torpedo tubes of the preceding MAHAN Class. The FANNINGs were distinguished by a single pole mast instead of a tripod type, and by fully enclosed number one and two 5-inch gun houses that appeared on the later CRAVEN Class.

Standard displacement on the two FANNINGs was the obligatory 1500 tons (1361 MT) mandated by the London Naval Treaty of 1930. By the time armament upgrades were completed, standard displacement had risen to 1717 tons (1558 MT) and full load wartime displacement was a maximum 2329 tons (2113 MT). Her length was 341 feet 8 inches (104.1 M) and beam was 35 feet 6 inches (10.8 M). The draft was 9 feet 10 inches (3 M) light and 17 feet (5.2 M) in full war load condition. The FANNING Class' speed was 38 knots (43.8 MPH/70.4 KMH) and their endurance was 4350 nautical miles (5009 miles/8061 KM) at 20 knots (23 MPH/37.1 KMH).

FANNING (DD-385) and DUNLAP (DD-384) were constructed by United Dry Dock Co. of New York (later Bethlehem), Staten Island, New York and both were commissioned in 1937. Following training and work-up in the Atlantic, both ships joined Destroyer Division 8, Destroyer Squadron 4 at San Diego, California. DUNLAP became the Division's flagship and retained this honor when Division 8 moved with the Pacific Fleet from San Diego to Pearl Harbor, Hawaii in 1940.

The FANNINGs were armed with five 5-inch (12.7 cm)/38 dual-purpose guns with the two forward (number one and two) mounts fully enclosed and the remaining three open, to save top weight. Four water-cooled 0.50 caliber (12.7MM) machine guns rounded out the armament. By 1942, the 0.50 machine guns were landed in favor of 20MM Oerlikon cannon and the number three 5-inch mount was replaced by a pair of twin 40MM Bofors cannon. Anti-aircraft armament upgrades continued until a maximum of eight 20MM in single mounts and four 40MM cannon in twin mounts were installed. Three Mk 14 or Mk 15 quad torpedo launchers were mounted: one on the centerline, and the other two along the port and starboard sides. Two depth charge roller tracks with seven depth charges each were mounted on the fantail. Four K-Guns – two each on the after deck side – completed the anti-submarine armament.

Both ships operated in the Pacific during World War Two and usually operated in concert with each other. FANNING earned four Battle Stars and DUNLAP six Battle Stars for their flags. Following the war, their careers were ended as they were sold for scrap.

USS DUNLAP (DD-384) was constructed by United Dry Dock, New York and launched on 18 April 1936. Following commissioning in 1937, she joined Destroyer Division 8 as the flagship. DUNLAP and FANNING (DD-385) were two odd sisters that resembled the MAHAN Class, but each had a pole mast instead of a tripod and the two forward 5-inch (12.7 CM) guns were fully enclosed instead of being semi-enclosed. (Floating Drydock)

A quarter stern view of DUNLAP off Staten Island, New York in the late 1930s. The depth charge roller tracks are fitted to the fantail and the starboard side fender that protected the propeller from wharf strikes is just forward on the hull. The aft superstructure area contained the 5-inch open mounts and aft steering position. (National Archives)

The Number Three starboard waist torpedo launcher fires off a 21-inch Mk 15 anti-ship torpedo during a practice run on 3 July 1942. The Number One centerline launcher is also positioned to make a launch. There were rare instances during World War Two when US destroyers launched torpedoes during battle. The gun mount just below the torpedo-handling crane lacks the 20MM Oerlikon cannon. (National Archives)

Mk 14/15 Quad Torpedo Launcher

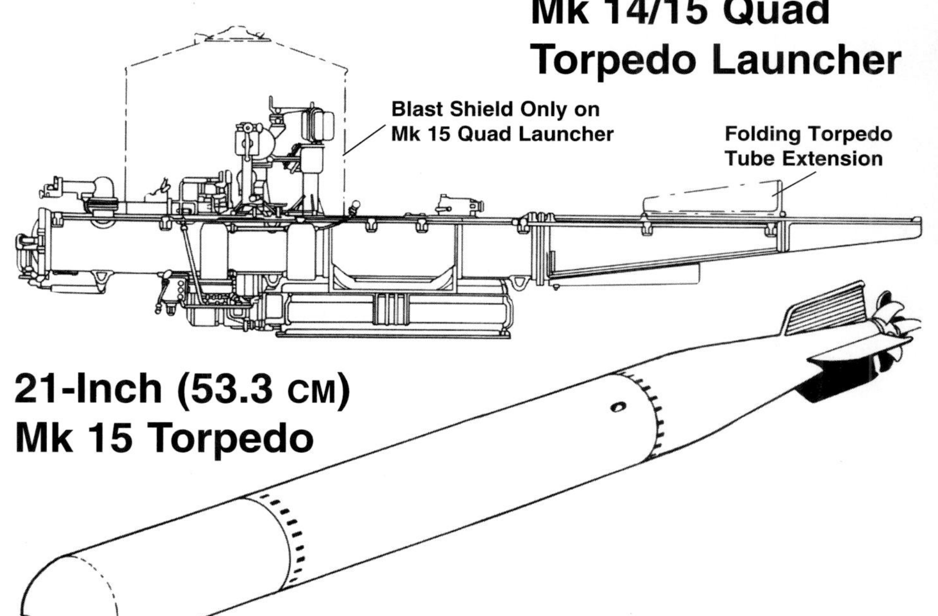

21-Inch (53.3 CM) Mk 15 Torpedo

DUNLAP's crew recovers an Mk 15 practice torpedo from the ocean on 3 July 1942. The 21-inch (53.3 CM) Mk 15 torpedo was 24 feet (7.3 M) long and had an 800-pound (363 KG) TNT (Torpex) warhead. This weapon had a range of 15,000 yards (13,716 M) and a speed of over 45 MPH (72.4 KMH). DUNLAP and FANNING were each armed with three quad torpedo tubes: one each on either side of the deck and one on the centerline. (National Archives)

35

DUNLAP passes close astern of the carrier ENTERPRISE (CV-6) while operating near Hawaii on 8 April 1942. The Task Force charged with conducting the Doolittle Raid on Japan was centered on the carriers HORNET (CV-8) and ENTERPRISE and they departed Pearl Harbor on that day. Deck crews are spotting a Douglas SBD Dauntless from Bombing Squadron Six (VB-6) on ENTERPRISE's aft fight deck. (National Archives)

DUNLAP is off the Mare Island Navy Yard on 10 May 1942, following a refitting after the Doolittle Raid on Japan the previous month. She is now armed with four 5-inch/38 guns and five 20MM cannon in single mounts, plus three quad 21-inch torpedo launchers. K-Gun depth charge launchers have been fitted to the deck just below the Number Four (ex-Number Five) 5-inch gun mount. (National Archives)

DUNLAP refuels at sea from the aircraft carrier SARATOGA (CV-3) on 26 March 1944. She is camouflaged in Measure 21, the Navy Blue System that was adopted for the Pacific War Zone. A pair of quad Bofors 40MM anti-aircraft guns has replaced the Number Three 5-inch mount. DUNLAP was acting as plane guard and anti-aircraft screen for SARATOGA during a sweep in the central Pacific. (National Archives)

A port quarter stern view of DUNLAP leaving Pearl Harbor, Hawaii in 1942. She is equipped with fantail mounted depth charge roller tracks, her aft 5-inch/38 open gun mounts, and her depth charge throwers (K-Guns). DUNLAP is camouflaged in Measure 11, the Sea Blue Scheme. She was awarded six Battle Stars for her service in the Pacific during World War Two. (National Archives)

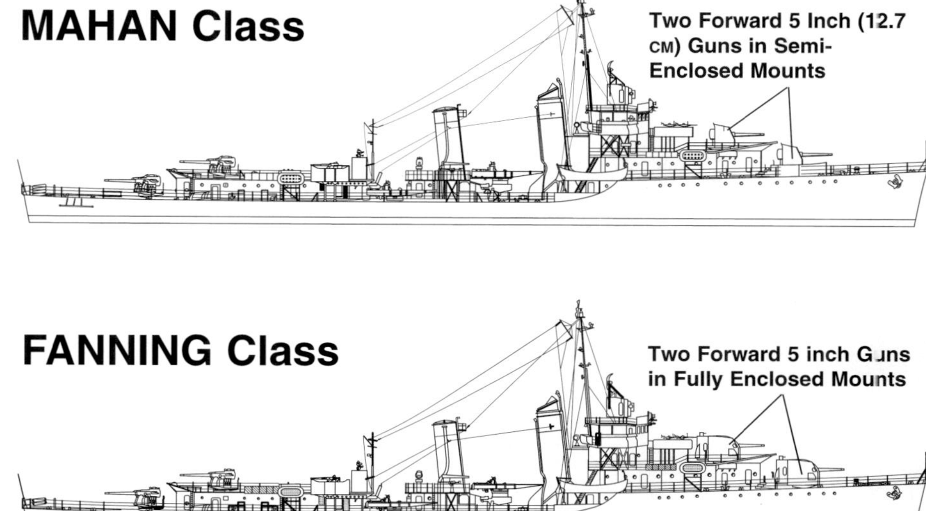

USS FANNING (DD-385) was the class leader and she was also built by United Dry Dock, New York and launched on 18 September 1936. She is painted in Measure 3, the Light Gray Scheme that was considered the standard 'peacetime' camouflage paint design. (National Archives)

(Below) FANNING escorts the carrier ENTERPRISE during the Doolittle Raid on Japan in April of 1942. The bridge roof is fitted with a canvas windscreen to protect the lookouts and observers. FANNING was awarded four Battle Stars for her service in the Pacific. (Naval Historical Center)

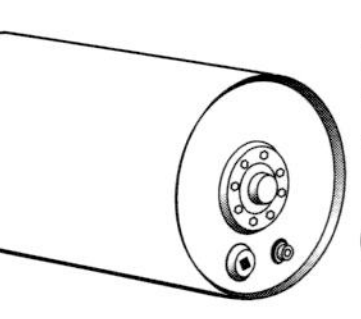

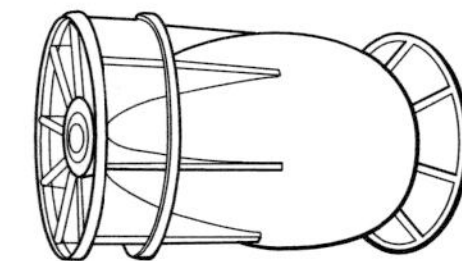

Depth Charge Roller Track

K-Gun with Depth Charge

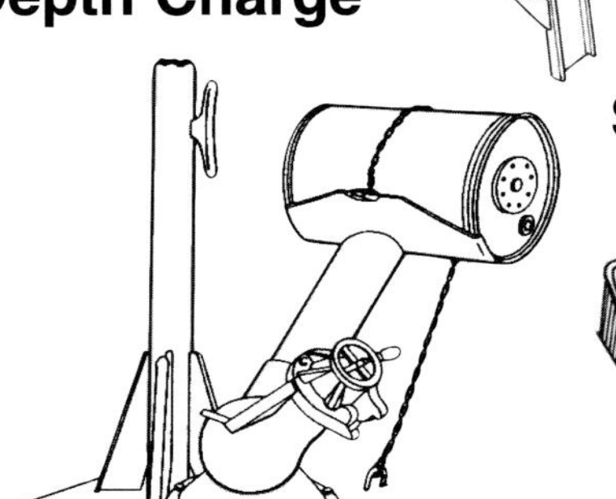

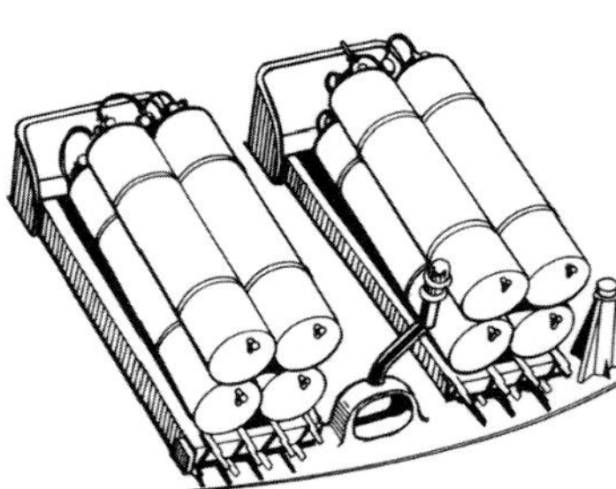

CRAVEN Class

The ten CRAVEN Class vessels ordered in 1934 were built to fill out the balance of the quota of 1500-ton (1361 MT) destroyers authorized by the 1930 London Naval Treaty. Following a basic design by the Bethlehem Company, they carried the most torpedo tubes ever fitted to a US destroyer.

The CRAVEN Class was 341 feet 3 inches (104 M) in length, with a beam of 34 feet 8 inches (10.6 M). Draft was rated at 13 feet 5 inches (4.1 M) standard and 17 feet (5.2 M) fully war loaded. The displacement was standard at 1500 tons as built, but anti-aircraft armament and electronic additions increased that to 1590 tons (1442 MT) and fully war loaded displacement was 2410 tons (2186 MT). No armor was fitted to the deck or any other sensitive areas, as in all earlier destroyer classes.

Only four 5-inch (12.7 CM)/38 caliber dual-purpose guns were fitted, with two fully enclosed forward guns and two open aft guns. This reduced gun armament allowed sixteen 21-inch (53.3 CM) torpedo tubes to be installed in four quad mounts on the main deck between the trunked stack and the after superstructure. Four 0.50 caliber (12.7MM) Browning machine guns were originally fitted for anti-aircraft protection, but British experiences in the Atlantic prompted a change to more powerful and longer range weapons. Up to eight 20MM Oerlikon cannon and a twin 40MM Bofors cannon were emplaced as they became available instead of the higher rate, but less efficient 0.50 caliber weapon.

The stern area was occupied with two depth charge roller tracks and smoke generating units outboard of each track. Four K-Gun depth charge throwers were placed to port and starboard of the aft superstructure. These were augmented by depth charge roller loader racks on the fantail. The depth charges were depth set and deployed at the direction of the sonar operators. Two types of depth charges were employed, the Mk 6 and 8 'Ash Can' types and the Mk 9 and 14 'Fast Sinking' types.

In 1942, the SC air-search radar was added atop the foremast to increase early detection of incoming enemy aircraft. SG surface-search radar to detect enemy ships and increase navigation efficiency during adverse weather conditions was fitted by early 1943. The 40MM cannon were directed by either the Mk 51 optical director or the radar controlled Mk 52 director.

Power for the CRAVENs came from four Yarrow boilers and twin Bethlehem turbines providing 50,000 SHP in CRAVEN (DD-382) and GRIDLEY (DD-380). The other eight ships in this class had four Babcock and Wilcox boilers and twin General Electric turbines generating 49,000 SHP. Speed was rated at 38.5 knots (44.3 MPH/71.3 KMH) for all of the class. Its range was 6500 miles (10,460 KM) at 12 knots (13.8 MPH/22.2 KMH) with onboard fuel of 525 tons (476 MT). Both CRAVEN and GRIDLEY were assigned to the Atlantic in 1945 and they had two of the torpedo tube mounts beached in favor of increased 20MM cannon.

The CRAVEN Class suffered three losses during their service in the Pacific War Zone. One Japanese aerial torpedo hit JARVIS (DD-393) on 8 August 1942, while she operated off Guadalcanal. Her damage control party was able to stabilize the ship and JARVIS was towed to Lunga Point where all unnecessary topside equipment – including her torpedo tubes, ship's boats, and life rafts – were beached. She then set sail to Australia for repairs. Caught in the open sea by the Japanese destroyer YUNANGI, JARVIS was again damaged, but sailed on. An American scout plane spotted JARVIS leaving a trail of fuel oil, but the Japanese had also spotted her and attacked. Following the intense aerial attack, she was left broken in two and sinking with the loss of all hands on 9 August 1942. JARVIS earned three Battle Stars for her Pacific service.

USS GRIDLEY (DD-380) was part of a new class of US destroyers built to answer the Japanese advantage in those ship types. The main armament was reduced to four of the 5-inch/38 dual-purpose naval guns in four single mounts, with the Number One and Two mounts fully enclosed and the Number Three and Four mounts completely open. (Floating Drydock)

GRIDLEY sails out of Bethlehem's Fore River Shipyard in Quincy, Massachusetts in 1937. She is painted in Measure 3, the Light Gray System. In order to make room on the deck for the four quad 21-inch torpedo launchers, a single oval shaped trunked stack replaced the twin stacks of earlier classes. A crow's nest fitted on the foremast provided a station for aerial and surface lookouts before the advent of radar. (Real War Photos)

USS CRAVEN (DD-382) was the Leader of the ten ship Class authorized in 1934. The Bethlehem 'house flag' flies at the top of her foremast as she make 15.19 knots (17.5 MPH/28 KMH) off of Rockland, Maine during trials on 5 August 1937. Following trials, training, and commissioning, CRAVEN joined Destroyer Division 11 of Battle Force, Destroyers at San Diego, California. (Naval Historical Center)

The second loss occurred just two weeks later, when BLUE (DD-387) was struck by two Japanese torpedoes on 22 August 1942. The damage was so severe that it was decided to allow the destroyer to sink into Savo Sound, the Solomons. All watertight doors were opened allowing the sea to claim the gallant ship. BLUE earned five Battle Stars for her flag in the Pacific Theater. The third and final loss occurred off of Cape Cretin, New Guinea on 3 October 1943, when a single torpedo struck HENLEY (DD-391). This occurred after she avoided two other torpedoes fired by the Japanese submarine Ro-108. The US destroyer escort ENGLAND (DE-635) sank Ro-108 and five of her sisters on 26 May 1944. HENLEY earned four Battle Stars for her flag for her service in the Pacific.

The CRAVEN Class all served with distinction during the battles in the Pacific. The seven survivors were all sold and scrapped by 1947. Both MUGFORD (DD-389) and RALPH TALBOT (DD-390) were used during the Bikini Atoll atomic bomb tests (Operation CROSSROADS) in 1946 and scuttled soon afterwards, thus ending the CRAVENs' careers.

A port quarter stern view of CRAVEN in 1944 reveals the smoke generators and roller tracks on the fantail and the two 5-inch (12.7 CM)/38 dual-purpose mounts. CRAVEN appears to be prepared to enter a dry dock, since her hull is marked with vertical lines along the frames. The aft superstructure is fitted with a splinter shield to protect the two single mount 20MM Oerlikon cannon. (US Navy)

The Number One 5-inch/38 dual-purpose enclosed gun mount on the deck of BAGLEY (DD-386) while she was moored at the Norfolk Navy Yard, Portsmouth, Virginia following a refit on 6 January 1938. The 5-inch gun had a muzzle velocity of 2600 feet (792 M) per second, a maximum range of 18,200 yards (16,642 M), and maximum altitude of 37,200 feet (11,339 M) at an 85° angle. The gun could be used against surface targets and aerial targets using proximity-fused rounds. (Naval Historical Center)

USS BLUE (DD-387) is moored outboard of USS RALPH TALBOT (DD-390) at the Mare Island Navy Yard on 11 April 1942. Both have Mk 33 fire control atop the bridge and new 20MM mounts and ready ammunition service lockers just forward of the bridge. These ships are camouflaged in Measure 11, the Sea Blue System. The bridge windows on BLUE have been modified by reducing their size as compared to RALPH TALBOT's. (National Archives)

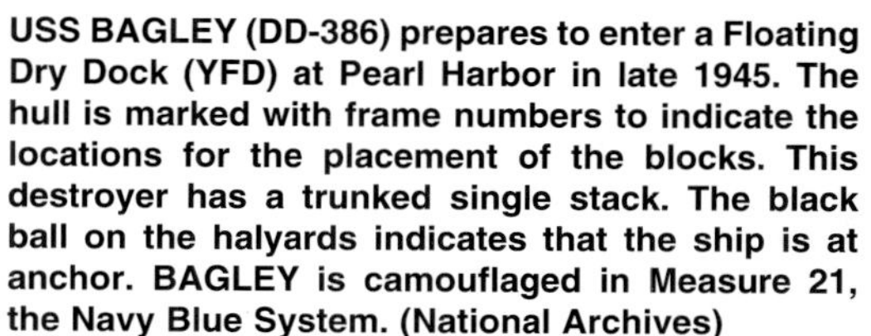

USS BAGLEY (DD-386) prepares to enter a Floating Dry Dock (YFD) at Pearl Harbor in late 1945. The hull is marked with frame numbers to indicate the locations for the placement of the blocks. This destroyer has a trunked single stack. The black ball on the halyards indicates that the ship is at anchor. BAGLEY is camouflaged in Measure 21, the Navy Blue System. (National Archives)

BAGLEY (DD-386) is off the Mare Island Navy Yard on 28 April 1944. She is camouflaged in Measure 32/1D, the Medium Pattern System, following a refit. The modifications included the addition of a twin Bofors 40MM anti-aircraft cannon just forward of the Number Three 5-inch open mount on the aft superstructure. BAGLEY was one of the few CRAVEN Class ships armed with the 40MM cannon. (National Archives)

BLUE transfers casualties to a Landing Craft Personnel, Large (LCP[L]) in Savo Sound, the Solomons on 22 August 1942. This occurred following her torpedoing by the Japanese destroyer KAWAKAZE. BLUE refused to sink and was scuttled by her crew and 5-inch rounds fired from HENLEY (DD-391). She was camouflaged in Measure 21, the Navy Blue System. BLUE was awarded five Battle Stars for her short nine months of combat in the Pacific. (National Archives)

USS HELM (DD-388) sails out of Norfolk Navy Yard, Portsmouth, Virginia in 1937 painted in Measure 3, the Light Gray System. Following her service in Atlantic Squadron 1 with Carrier Division 2, she transferred to Pearl Harbor and joined Destroyer Division 11, Destroyer Squadron 6. HELM is armed with four 5-inch/38 dual-purpose guns and four quad 21-inch torpedo tubes. (National Archives)

Following training and commissioning, HELM was assigned to the newly formed Atlantic Squadron 1 on 1 October 1939 and served with Carrier Division 2 in the Caribbean. Her Number One and Two mounts were painted a dark gray and the main, fore, and after masts were given the 'barber pole' treatment, as well as on the whistle and siren pipes on the stack. The Germans similarly painted a few of the gun mounts on their destroyers in the late 1930s. (National Archives)

(Above Left) HELM is off the Mare Island Navy Yard on 26 February 1942, camouflaged in Measure 21, the Navy Blue System. She has just undergone a period of refit and modifications, with the addition of a pair of 20MM cannon in the bridge area and on the aft superstructure to increase anti-aircraft protection. The majority of the hull side portholes are plated and painted over. (National Archives)

(Above) HELM closes up on another ship to receive mail and a new movie. She is camouflaged in Measure 31/1D, the Dark Pattern System that utilized Haze Gray (5-H), Ocean Gray (5-O), and Dull Black (BK) paint. HELM has SC air-search radar atop the foremast, SG surface-search radar just below it, and IFF antennas on the main yard. (Naval Historical Center)

(Left) HELM comes alongside the escort carrier MAKIN ISLAND (CVE-93) to take on some fuel following a raid on Japanese positions on Iwo Jima in February of 1945. HELM was acting as a screen for the escort carrier Task Force during the 'Island Hopping' campaign. She was awarded 11 Battle Stars for her service in the Pacific during World War Two. (National Archives)

(Above) USS MUGFORD (DD-389) is off of Boston Navy Yard, Massachusetts on 25 October 1937. She is painted in Measure 3, the Light Gray System that was the standard 'peacetime' scheme. She later sailed to the Pacific and was assigned as flagship of Destroyer Division 11, at Pearl Harbor. During the Japanese attack on Pearl Harbor on 7 December, MUG-FORD was credited with shooting down one enemy aircraft. (National Archives)

(Above Right) MUGFORD is off the Mare Island Navy Yard on 28 April 1944. She is camouflaged in a Measure 31/1D, the Dark Pattern System drawn especially for destroyers and some light cruisers (CLs). MUGFORD carries SC air-search and SG surface-search radar antenna on the foremast and IFF antennas on the yards. The Mk 33 fire control director is fitted with FD ranging radar to increase the anti-aircraft guns' effectiveness. (National Archives)

(Right) MUGFORD sails off the Mare Island Navy Yard with all of her quad 21-inch torpedo tubes swung out for action on 28 February 1945. She is camouflaged in Measure 22, the Graded System. During a one and a half year period, MUGFORD was camouflaged in Measure 21, 22, and 31/1D schemes. A smoke generator is fitted to the fantail just to the right of the starboard depth charge roller track. (National Archives)

MUGFORD moves slowly off the Mare Island Navy Yard following a refit on 28 February 1945. She is camouflaged in Measure 22, the Graded System that utilized Navy Blue (5-N) and Haze Gray (5-H) paint. Her foremast is fitted with SC air-search and SG surface-search radar antennas. MUGFORD is now fitted with only two ship's boats in a weight saving measure. (National Archives)

RALPH TALBOT (DD-390) sails in Hawaiian waters camouflaged in Measure 21, the Navy Blue System in January of 1943. Additional 20MM Oerlikon cannon are now fitted around the bridge area, in bandstands around the stack area, and on the aft superstructure. The foremast contains SC air-search radar at the top and SG surface-search radar just below at the yard. (National Archives)

RALPH TALBOT in San Francisco Bay camouflaged in Measure 31/1D, the Dark Pattern System that was generally employed in the Pacific in May of 1944. She is fitted with SC air-search and SG surface-search radar on the foremast and FD fire control radar on the Mk 33 fire control director. A US Coast Guard flag is unfurled on a ship to RALPH TALBOT's right. She was awarded 12 Battle Stars for her service in the Pacific. (Naval Historical Center)

Looking highly sleek, USS HENLEY (DD-391) cruises off of the Mare Island Navy Yard on 26 February 1942. She is returning to her duty as flagship for Destroyer Division 11 at Pearl Harbor. She is camouflaged in Measure 21, the Navy Blue System. HENLEY was sunk while operating off of New Guinea on 3 October 1943. She was awarded four Battle Stars for her actions in the Pacific. (Naval Historical Center)

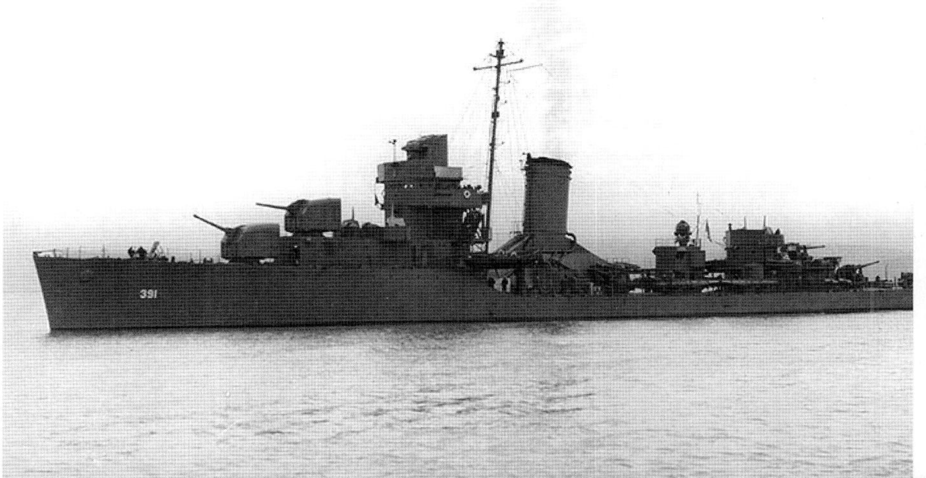

HENLEY is moored to a staging wharf at the Mare Island Navy Yard on 1 October 1937, during her fitting out period following her commissioning the previous 14 August. She soon sailed to Pearl Harbor and was the first destroyer to open fire on the attacking Japanese force. HENLEY shot down one aircraft with her 0.50 caliber (12.7MM) machine guns and shared credit with another destroyer for another aircraft. The Navy Jack flies at the jack staff while she is in port. (Naval Historical Center)

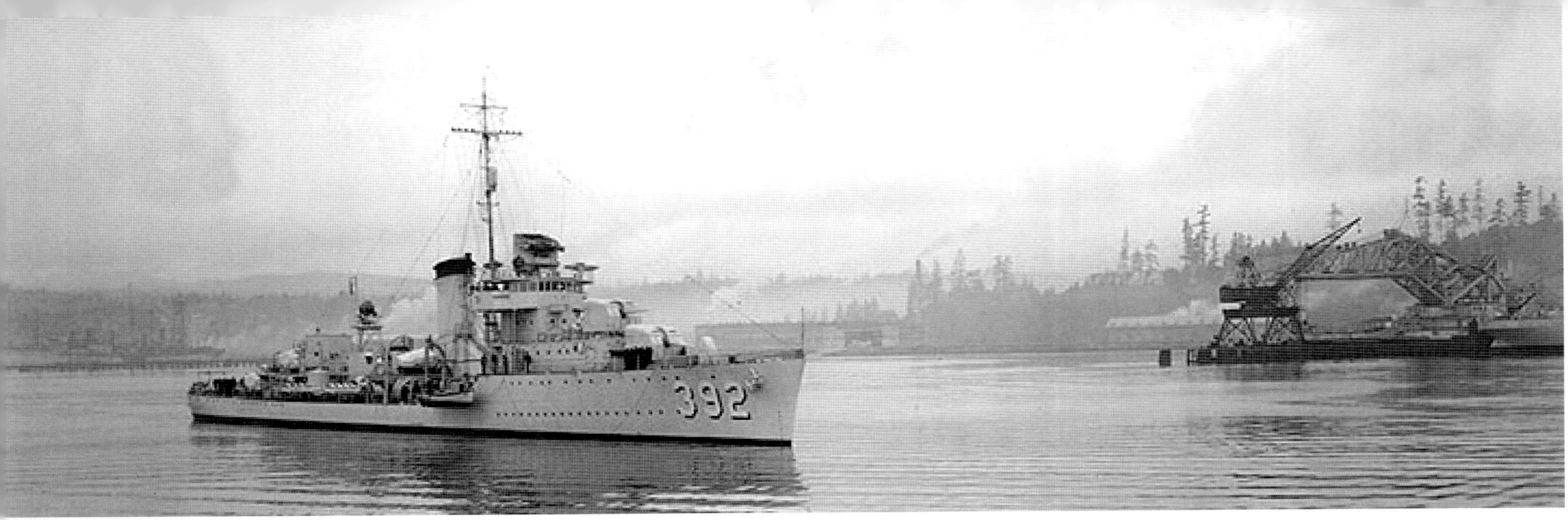

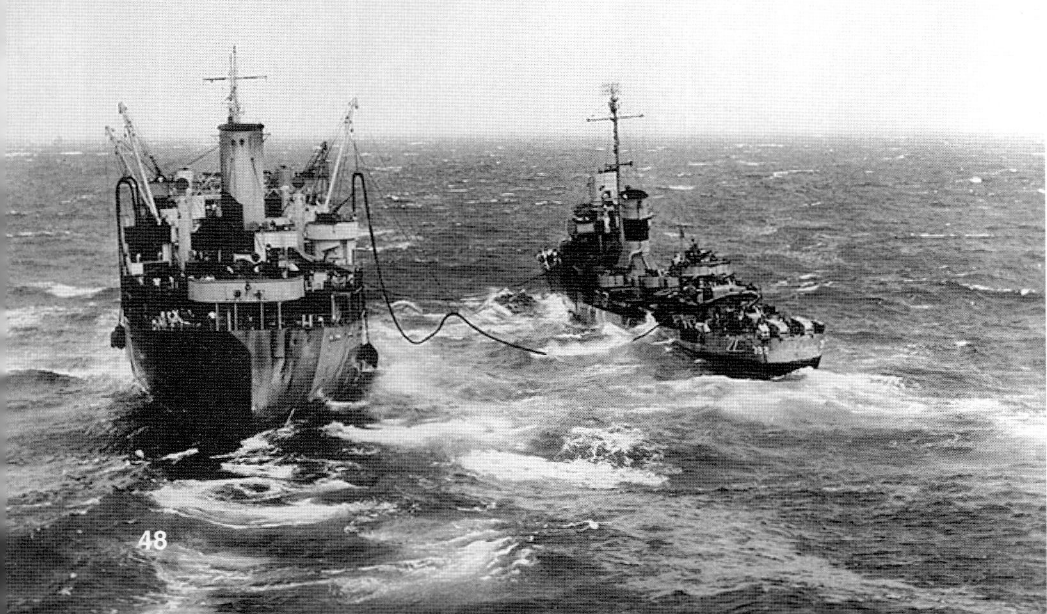

USS PATTERSON (DD-392) returns to the Puget Sound Navy Yard, Washington in fresh Measure 3, the Light Gray System, paint on 22 December 1937. She would spend time training off the West Coast before sailing to the Caribbean for additional training. PATTERSON returned to the Pacific to join Destroyer Division 8 in 1940. (Naval Historical Center)

PATTERSON refuels at sea from a US Navy tanker (AO) during the Lingayen Gulf operations in January of 1945. She is camouflaged in Measure 32/2C, the Light Pattern System and was the only 1500-ton (1361 MT) destroyer to carry that scheme. The two ships are keeping a respectable distance from each other due to the high sea condition in the gulf. (Naval Historical Center)

SG Radar Antenna

SC-3 Radar Antenna

Mk 12 Radar Antenna Atop Mk 37 Gun Director

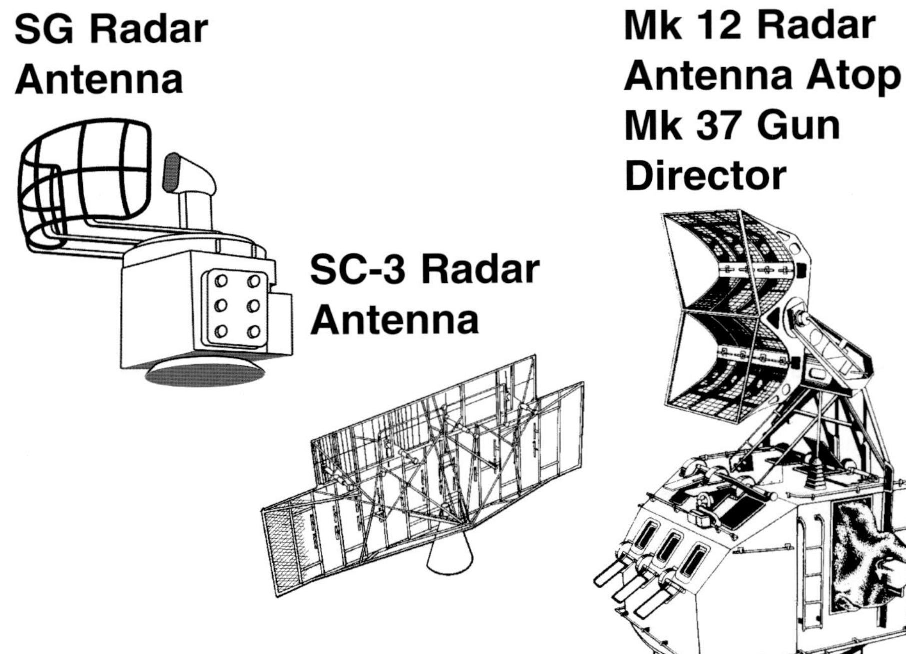

PATTERSON approaches HMAS CANBERRA from the stern as BLUE comes along side to assist the crew of the fatally damaged Australian cruiser off Guadalcanal. This took place at approximately 0630 on the morning of 9 August 1942, following the battle of Savo Island. The US lost three cruisers during this engagement. BLUE herself was sunk by a Japanese torpedo in Savo Sound just 13 days later, on 22 August. (National Archives)

USS JARVIS (DD-393) is off the Puget Sound Navy Yard following her commissioning in December of 1937. She is painted in Measure 3, the Light Gray System. She is fitted with 0.50 caliber machine guns to either side of her Mk 33 optical fire control director atop the bridge. JARVIS was sunk off of Tulagi in the Solomons on 9 August 1942, following concentrated attacks by Japanese air and naval forces. (Naval Historical Center)

More Ocean Escorts
from squadron/signal publications

4008 Fletcher DDs

4011 Destroyer Escorts

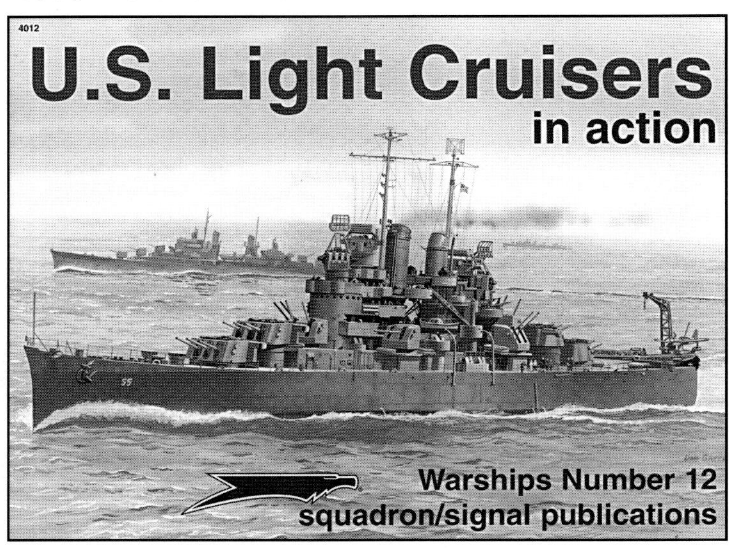

4012 US Light Cruisers

4019 US Flush Deck Destroyers

For a complete listing of squadron/signal books, go to www.squadron.com